Kelleys of the Outrigger

KELLEYS
of the Outrigger

By John W. McDermott

Edited by B.L. Hughes
ORAFA Publishing Company, Inc.
Honolulu, Hawaii

Published 1990
ORAFA Publishing Company, Inc.
Honolulu, Hawaii 96815

Designed by Hill and Knowlton/
Communications-Pacific, Inc.
Illustrations by Elizabeth A. Chapman
Printed by Edwards Brothers, Michigan

ISBN: 0-912273-19-4 (paperback edition)
ISBN: 0-912273-18-6 (hardcover edition)
ISBN: 0-912273-20-8 (deluxe hardcover edition)

Library of Congress Cataloging in Publication Data

McDermott, John W., 1920 -
    KELLEYS OF THE OUTRIGGER
    Includes index, photographs, sketches.
    1. Kelly, Roy and Estelle. 2. Hawaii – Biography. 3. Hawaii –
    Development of tourism in Waikiki. 4. Preeminent "Mom & Pop"
    business team – Hawaii. I. Title. 90-61129

Dedicated to all the people -- the Kelley family, their friends and employees, past and present, the members of the travel industry -- who gave so generously of their time to interviews, answering queries and volunteering stories. The result, I hope, is the preservation of a unique chapter in Waikiki history that might otherwise have been lost.

CONTENTS

Four sections of photographs follow pages
18, 50, 66, and 210

FOREWORD

This is your classic Horatio Alger tale.

The child raised in a threadbare California family environment works his way through school, suffers a family divorce, supports his mother, becomes an architect, lands in Honolulu with just a few dollars in his pocket the day the stock market crashed in 1929, crafts a successful professional career while operating a profitable sideline of building and renting apartments, goes blind at the beginning of World War II, has his eyesight partially restored, returns to work, survives a crushing auto accident, but, in spite of all adversities, becomes Waikiki's largest landlord — 21 hotels with 7,500 rooms — and builds a billion dollar empire.

Roy Cecil Kelley became a visitor industry leader through the Horatio Alger principles of seven-day work weeks, dogged dedication and unswerving perseverance. Those were the easy principles.

What made the difference in the Kelley success saga was diligent bifocal vision of a constant eye — his good eye — on the guest while never losing sight of the cigar box that held the day's cash.

In the best storybook tradition, his closest colleague and burden equalizer was his indefatigable hard-working wife, Estelle Foote Kelley, who shared a shoulder-to-shoulder role in the family climb to modest fame and sizable fortune.

This is their story, recalled while pouring over cherished scrapbooks and photo albums and yellowed newspaper and magazine clippings with Roy and Estelle Kelley. It is a story expanded by revealing interviews with family and friends, colleagues and competitors, employees and suppliers.

After such research, the reasons for the growth of the Kelley empire become obvious. The ability to build at a low cost. The talent to operate with the lowest overhead costs. The constant attendance to the business at hand. And a knack for attention to detail.

But, when asked, Roy Kelley lays his success at the feet of the two women who have always been there for him, his wife and Lady Luck.

And the harder they worked, the luckier they became.

There was no doubt that Roy was the captain of the ship, commanding the deck in the strong wind, setting every inch of canvas to go faster and farther. But Estelle was at once the ballast and the steady hand on the tiller, making sure that the ship remained upright and stayed on course.

I arrived in Hawaii the same year the Kelleys opened the Edgewater Hotel, their third. It was not long after the hotel opened that tongues wagged of Roy Kelley's operational habit of standing by the front desk negotiating *very* flexible room rates directly with off-the-street guests ("whatever the traffic would bear" was the rumor), of personally bellhopping luggage if necessary, and of keeping his cash in a cigar box. Such stories were the stuff of knee-slapping gossip.

A couple of decades later, when the knee slapping had changed to admiring hand clapping and the Kelleys numbered their hotel rooms in the thousands, I attended the 1970 national convention of the American Society of Travel Agents in Amsterdam. The Kelleys were registered also.

My interest in ASTA was as a partner in an advertising agency whose travel clients included Henry J. Kaiser who built the Hawaiian Village Hotel (now the Hilton Hawaiian Village), the Sheraton Hotels in Hawaii, the Hawaii Visitors Bureau, Continental Airlines, Aloha Airlines, and British Overseas Airways Corporation (predecessor to British Airways), among others.

In the course of various travel-oriented meetings I had met Roy and Estelle but, at best, we were casual acquaintances. Together, we have experienced the growth of tourism from a visitor count of 50,000 in 1951, my first year in Hawaii, to a visitor count well in excess of 6,000,000 in 1989.

In Amsterdam, that autumn day in 1970, Roy and Estelle and their younger daughter, Pat, boarded a ship for a day cruise on the Zuider Zee. I had also signed aboard and, as people from the same town tend to do when they meet in a foreign environment, we fell into natural conversation.

Roy, then as now, was gray of hair. A tall, somewhat heavy man, he wore thick glasses and used a cane which detracted not at all from an unconscious authoritative manner of walk. His mantle of command was belied by a manner which was inherently simple. Straight forward in conversation, his comments were sprinkled with chuckles and boisterous laughter. A genial man without pretense. None. Ever.

He liked to tell stories, to hear jokes, break into snatches of remembered songs, and to relate his observations.

"These restaurant operators," I remember him saying during our cruise, "they are all the same. Once one gets a little success with a restaurant, he buys a Mercedes, starts to play golf, leaves the maitre d' job to a hired hand, and the restaurant goes to hell, and he loses it."

Estelle Kelley was and is the perfect counter balance for Roy, a gentle lady, a genial companion. She has a lovely smile. It is hard to determine whether it starts at the corners of her mouth or in her hazel eyes and then is reflected through glasses to the rest of her face. She seemed so petite beside the robust Roy. Petite she might have been in stature, and soft of speech, but she had a towering reputation for speaking her mind, fearlessly and firmly correcting her husband when she thought it necessary.

Today Roy Kelley, retired from all hotel operations, sits under an overhang beside the pool at the Outrigger Village Hotel. Some of the flock of white pigeons he feeds daily swagger proprietarily around him. A glass of ice water sits by his hand.

He had been for his daily six a.m. swim at Gray's Beach in front of the Halekulani Hotel where a fresh underwater spring prevents coral growth and warms the sea water. It is a sight to behold to see this Pied Piper of the Pigeons leading his flock down to the sea on Kalia Road.

He has had his breakfast.

By nine o'clock Estelle has joined him and, here in the shade by the pool, they read and talk and hold court with a wide assortment of friends who wander by. She is somewhat subdued. She no longer takes the early morning swim because a serious heart condition created the need for a pacemaker.

Behind them are three offices. One belongs to Ruth Harada, Roy's secretary for forty years; another is for his personal accountant where Roy indulges in his single passionate hobby, playing the stock market. The third room is furnished with a drafting table and swivel stool and a humble cot where Roy often naps. Its walls are lined from floor to ceiling with cardboard boxes filled with commercial records of transactions.

Each office is simple, plain. No frills. No pretenses.

Next door, at the Outrigger Waikiki Tower, the Kelleys occupy a two-story penthouse accessible only by private elevator.

Roy takes pride in its outdoor garden. He shows the visitor the flowers, the green lawn, the fishpond and waterfall, and the Chinese Moon Gate, a familiar architectural appendage of an earlier Hawaii era. He walks his visitor around the perimeter of the penthouse, identifying the neighboring buildings, most of them being Outrigger Hotels.

The living room of the penthouse is basically American Comfortable, devoid of *House and Garden* decorator touches. Seated on a deep-cushioned couch, Roy turns the pages of the family album, while Estelle provides counterpart comments from the sideline.

We'll pick it up there.

CHAPTER ONE

*Childhoods —
California Orange Groves
and Jersey City*

A faded black and white photograph of a horse and buggy in front of a simple wood framed house in the middle of an orange grove is the first entry in the Kelley family album.

The buggy's occupants are a man in coat and tie, his lady, an adult daughter and son, and a subteen lad.

"Yes," says Roy, "that's my father, Lewis Franklin Kelley, and my mother, Minnie Mae, my brother, Amos, and my sister, Iva."

"Actually, his half brother and half sister," injects Estelle. "His father lost his first wife and married her first cousin. They came from Arkansas. There was Indian blood on that side of the family. Cherokee."

John Roy Kelley was Roy's grandfather. His wife was half Cherokee. The grandfather sired fifteen children but never saw the last five children because he went blind.

"That was a working horse and buggy," Roy picks up. "We had a barn in back. No milk cow. But chickens. We always had chickens. There was a lot next door which my father cleared and built a house on, then rented out.

"I was born on August 31, 1905 in Redlands, California where we lived in this house in the middle of the orange country. It was just a little community in those days. Agricultural. Orange groves all around us. Everywhere, there were orange groves.

"My father became a concrete mason and built many of the sidewalks and curbs in Redlands, California. You can still see 'LF Kelley' imprinted in the old Redlands sidewalks. The big thing though was making water flumes and pipes for the surrounding orange groves — until one winter the area was hit by a gigantic frost that ruined the orange industry."

That disaster spelled the end of the Kelley masonry business, and of their life in Redlands. The family moved to San Diego where Lewis Franklin, the father, helped construct buildings for the Panama/California Exposition of 1915-16 in Balboa Park. When that work was finished, the family moved to urban Los Angeles.

"We lived by the skin of our teeth," recalls Roy Kelley. "But some way or another we always got by. I always had enough to eat. I have no memory of wanting, or needing, money at all. We were used to doing without it."

His strongest memory is as a victim of the influenza epidemic of 1918. That tragedy resulted in the loss of life of more than half a million Americans, the most devastating epidemic in world history. His mother successfully nursed the thirteen-year-old back to health.

Later, still in his early teens, his father and mother separated. She became a professional children's nurse for several prominent Los Angeles families while Roy boarded near Westlake and attended Los Angeles High School.

Another well thumbed picture in the family album is of Estelle's paternal grandmother and grandfather, George Henry Foote, in Newfoundland, where he was a ship builder.

Her father, George Pearce Foote, moved to New Jersey with Hannah, his new bride, in 1903. Hannah said she wouldn't marry him unless he promised to move to the United States.

Estelle was born in the family home in Jersey City where an extra room was rented out to Uncle Matt, her mother's brother.

Her mother was known for her rich red hair. "Not carrot red," remembers Estelle, "but more of a Titian red. It was full and luxurious and fell down to her shoulders. One time she broke her hand and my father had to comb her hair. He combed it with long, loving strokes again and again — like they did in those days — and, I recall him saying to her, 'You know, I always wanted to do this.'"

Estelle's home birth was not recorded, an oversight which later created problems when she applied for her first passport.

Her earliest childhood memories are of going to the neighborhood grocery store and playing children's games such as tic-tac-toe and hopscotch. She finished grammar school and a year of high school in Jersey City before the family moved to Los Angeles when she was thirteen years old.

"My sister had polio. We knew it in those days as infantile paralysis. One leg was crippled as a result. Well, we heard about a surgeon in Los Angeles who had a reputation of being able to correct a condition such as hers. The whole family moved out to Los Angeles so my sister could have the operation. It was successful.

"My father bought a lot in Los Angeles at Vernon and Vermont Avenues and built a house. My mother always insisted on having an extra room in the house which she could rent out."

The heritage of building to rent were ingrained characteristics of both the Kelley and the Foote families.

Mr. Foote also built a vacation house in the mountains. A picture of a winsome Estelle Foote in a puttee-and-britches hiking outfit in the family album brought a smile to Roy's face.

Roy Kelley and Estelle Foote were half a semester apart at Los Angeles High School, but never met.

"If I had met her, I would have married her then," says Roy with obvious relish, looking at the hiking photograph.

Estelle continues, "I was supposed to go to Manual Arts High School but it was full so they offered me enrollment at either Polytechnic or Los Angeles High School. I didn't know what Polytechnic meant so I chose LA High even though it was way out of my district. LA High was new then and in the middle of the oat fields at the end of the streetcar line.

"On the East Coast, most of the girls went to high school for two and a half years only and then went to work as a typist or as a secretary.

"So in LA High I took a business course in addition to reading, writing and arithmetic ... things like that. I finished four years of high school, then when my mother found out that college was such a bargain in California, she sent me to college — UCLA. I think the cost was $12.50 a semester."

Tommy Perkins, who was to become a prominent Honolulu architect, was also a classmate of Roy and Estelle at Los Angeles High School and today remains a close friend of the couple.

The family album contains a bust shot of Roy in a ROTC school uniform. His regular features are handsome, serious, determined, an All American Jack Armstrong type.

Was he the ROTC commander?

"No," he laughs loudly. "I was a scared little boy in those days. I only made sergeant.

"LA High was a fine school." He remembers and booms out a school cheer:

"You can't beat LA High—

"Any old team

"Can work up steam—

"But you can't beat LA High."

The high school classes made periodic field trips to various business and professional offices and, after visiting an architect's office, Roy became intrigued with the idea of creating buildings on a drafting board.

Following graduation he enrolled in the University of Southern California's School of Architecture.

"I almost went to the University of California but they had a big fire up there so I went to Southern Cal."

Roy paid for his tuition and helped support his mother

by working from three p.m. until midnight as a Pacific Electric Railroad clerk.

He worked in the Lost and Found Office, made change, collected tokens, gave out information and, in the late hours between customers, he studied. He had no time for the college social life.

Roy Kelley graduated at the head of his class in 1927 and the family scrapbook contains his graduation announcement in a formal folder, together with his first calling card. It reads "Roy C. Kelley."

"I don't know where I got the money to have a card printed," he says staring at the faded pamphlet and card.

The memory of the University of Southern California sparks a song. Roy laughs and leans back and sings:

"Don't send my boy to Stanford, the dying mother said.

"Don't send my boy to Stanford. I'd rather see him dead.

"Send my boy to old SC, it's better than Cornell.

"Don't send my boy to Stanford, I'd see him first in hell."

He roars with extra pleasure probably because Richard, their first born, went to Stanford and Jeannie, their first daughter, went to Cornell.

Roy's first job was with a Beverly Hills architect named Flannery whose clients included William Randolph Hearst. As a result, Roy worked on a Santa Monica house where Marion Davies, Hearst's great and good friend, lived.

"I was not working on the Marion Davies house but on Bebe Daniels' house right next door," recalls Roy Kelley. "Daniels was a friend of Marion Davies. I think Hearst was also a friend of Daniels. Gets all mixed up there."

Then Roy heard about an opening for an architect at San Juan Capistrano where Ed Doheny, the scion of the oil-rich Doheny family, was developing a tract of houses as part of a new beach community. The marketing attraction was that all the houses were to be architect designed. Roy Kelley became the staff architect.

"There was nothing there but sand. The subdivision was next to the stream that came down from Santa Ana and that was all there was to it. The development was a total gamble."

Doheny's sales promotional gimmick was to hold "bean luncheons" for potential buyers. He transported prospects to the coastal property by bus, served the bean meal, then gave them a chance to buy the "real estate of a lifetime" at auction.

Roy's job included a bit of shilling. He sometimes called out, "Don't sell lot number 44. I have a buyer!"

How much did the job pay?

"Oh, about $100 a week."

Meanwhile, Estelle Foote's father gave her a Model T Ford roadster to drive to classes at the old UCLA campus.

She belonged to a small sorority and admits to having had a lot of boy friends. A newspaper clipping in the scrapbook shows her holding a lap full of chicks on a field trip. Estelle Foote was a cute little chick herself.

"I worked at school as a reader/tutor for different courses. Any course at the university where I got an 'A-plus' qualified me to be a reader. I was paid fifty cents an hour. One professor particularly, who was head of the geography department, had a soft spot in his heart for me and threw a lot of work my way. He was nice.

"I was very young and, even then, didn't look my age. Once I had a group of students at a reading session about me when a professor came in, looked around and wanted to know where the teacher was."

There was no sense of vanity — just fact — in her relating the incident.

Estelle graduated in 1927 from UCLA with a teacher's certificate. She couldn't find a job in the educational system and, while working as an assistant to a lawyer in a collection agency, she took night classes in law. This proved to be a most valuable asset later in Honolulu. She then went to work for the Los Angeles Police Department as a secretary.

"I remember my first job was copying down numbers from pawn tickets to try and trace stolen goods."

A mutual friend, Bert Conrad, brought Estelle and Roy together on a blind date to go to a stage play.

Estelle: "I don't remember the name of the play but I remember I liked him from the beginning. He paid a lot of attention to me."

Roy paid enough close attention to Estelle that they were married in May, 1929 at the Church of the Holy Faith, an Episcopalian church in Inglewood, California.

Roy: "I had a car then — it was called an American Beauty and it was made in Oakland. We drove north on our honeymoon and we were no sooner out of town that we got a speeding ticket. Cost me five dollars. Cash. I'm sure the policeman just put it in his pocket.

"The first place we stopped was Santa Rosa. We didn't have a hotel reservation and we couldn't find a room. Finally, we had to settle for what we called a drummer's room, a place where a salesman had space to spread out his samples and call customers in. The bed came out of the wall. Probably cost us five dollars a night."

Estelle interrupts. When we got to the California border, Roy pretended to make a big fuss about being scared to cross the line because, you see, he had never been out of the state before." The recall brought an added twinkle to her eyes.

Roy: "Went as far as the Columbia River. Real nice honeymoon. Sixty-one years ago."

They returned to the California seaside village of Capistrano, the same one the swallows return to year after year.

Roy had built a house on a lot given to him by Doheny which became their honeymoon home. He built another house on a lot next door for his mother.

He also designed a spacious open air gazebo overlooking the beach for the developer. The scrapbook contains a photo of the newlyweds in the gazebo. Recently, the city bought back the site from a private owner, restored the gazebo to the original Kelley design, and designated it as a public park.

Misfortune touched the lives of the newlyweds too soon. Young Doheny returned to the family mansion in Beverly

Hills one afternoon after work to be met by his male secretary with a gun in hand who fired on his employer. The shot was fatal. It not only killed Doheny, it killed the Capistrano project.

Roy, out of a job, couldn't find work in Los Angeles. He dropped by an office building in Hollywood at Fifth and Figueroa which was occupied by architectural firms. Through a friend working with one of the firms Roy learned that an architect in Honolulu, C. W. Dickey, was looking for a draftsman/designer.

"We exchanged cables and I was hired. Four days later we were on the *City of Los Angeles*, sailing for Honolulu.

"We weren't sure where Honolulu was. But we were young. We had our car, the American Beauty. And, maybe, somewhere around $100 in cash."

(A review of different yellowed press clippings revealed that the Kelleys landed with $10 in their pockets ... and $35 ... and $108.)

"Whatever it was, it wasn't much. By the time we paid the first month's rent, we were broke," remembers Roy.

The day the ship docked in Honolulu was September 13, 1929 — "Black Friday" — the day Wall Street collapsed and the United States slid into its worst depression.

The Kelleys had arrived in the Territory of Hawaii.

>   *In 1929, the Territory of Hawaii received 22,000 visitors. All visitors arrived by ship. There were three hotels: the Moana and the Royal Hawaiian in Waikiki, both owned and operated by the Matson Navigation Company, and the Alexander Young Hotel in downtown Honolulu.*

CHAPTER TWO

Prewar Honolulu ...
Pearl Harbor ...
Evacuation

Honolulu, in 1929, was the commercial center of a sugar-and-pineapple plantation economy which existed on all islands.

Gentlemen wore white linen suits.

"They had to be ironed every night," recalls Estelle.

No one locked a house or a car. There was free curbside parking available everywhere. Crime was nonexistent. Bills were paid every three months.

The tallest building was the slender, ten-story Aloha Tower facing the busy waterfront. There was no air-conditioning. Near the waterfront was Hotel Street, so named because hotels lined the street to take care of sailors attracted to the kind of business that sailors are interested in. The hotels were not for Mainland U.S.A. tourists.

The Pacific Club, utilizing the former mansion of Archibald Cleghorn who was a member of King Kalakaua's House of Lords and offering cottages for bachelors, and Oahu Country Club, a private golf club on slopes overlooking downtown Honolulu, were the social and sporting centers for the Caucasian political and economic elite.

Kalakaua Avenue, then and now the principal thoroughfare in Waikiki, was comparatively traffic free except for the streetcar whose rails occupied the middle of the street.

It was a peaceful time in the Hawaiian Islands. Everything in its place and everybody accepting their traditional roles in the society.

The Depression took over a year to reach Honolulu. When it did arrive, the effect was minimal on the architectural firm of C. W. Dickey. (His first name was Charles but everyone called him "C. W." or "Pop.") Dickey was well connected to the Territory's hierarchy and one of the most successful architects of his time.

As a result of Dickey's influence, Roy Kelley worked on many Hawaii buildings that are still considered architectural landmarks. Among them is the ecclesiastical stylistic Montague Hall at Punahou School and the nurses home at Queen's Hospital. The Spanish style of architecture, popular in Honolulu in the Twenties and Thirties, is evident in his Immigration Station on Ala Moana Boulevard. The Waikiki Theater, with its marvelously lofted ceiling speckled with stars and clouds, bears the touch of a Hollywood transplant.

Roy: "Some people have given me credit for the A & B (Alexander & Baldwin) building but, actually, all I did was the flowerpots."

The Kelleys' first home was a modest duplex cottage on Dewey Lane owned by the Vitousek family in a complex called the "Marigold Apartments." The cottage faced the beach where the Hilton Hawaiian Village now stands.

"We didn't have hot water," Estelle remembers, "we had an old wooden ice box that had to have a fresh block of ice each day. The water dripped out on the floor. Roy drilled a hole in the floor to let the water drip out into the sand. We paid $45 a month.

"It didn't take long to find out that there weren't many respectable jobs for women in Honolulu, particularly married women. So I had to get a temporary job here and a temporary job there.

"One day I was working at Kamehameha Schools giving boys their IQ tests. Several of us were correcting papers for fifty cents an hour. One of the girls was married to a local boy. She was a society girl from the East Coast who had to go to work for the first time in her life. She was a college graduate which was all the professional requirement any of us needed for the work we were doing.

"She came running in one day saying, 'If I had any legal experience, I could have gotten the most wonderful job.'

"I immediately perked up my ears because I had had experience as a legal secretary on the Mainland. I asked, 'Where is this job?'"

The job was with Judge James L. Coke who was appointed to the State Supreme Court by President Woodrow Wilson and reappointed by Franklin D. Roosevelt.

At one time Judge Coke served as a conservator for the minor heirs of the Campbell Estate and, later, became a Campbell Estate trustee.

Estelle went to work for the judge.

"He was a brilliant man who spoke fluent Hawaiian. He could sit down and dictate for two or three hours legal documents in simple English that the average citizen could understand and the document would be perfect, without any need to edit or change at all."

"Oh, yes," Roy remembers. "He and his wife were nice people. Eventually I designed their home up in Nuuanu. It was a lovely house on the stream. A beautiful home, if I say so myself."

The Kelleys used to drive downtown in the American Beauty and park by the library building.

"We had our lunch every day at the YWCA. It was about ninety cents. Damned expensive. That was our big meal of the day. Our only hobby on days off was to go tramping around the island."

"When I got pregnant," Estelle interrupts, "I gave Judge Coke notice and said I would be leaving at the end of the sixth month, but I waited until two months before Richard was born. You see, the money was very important to us. I had a big salary. I got $165 a month."

Pivotal Years—1932-1938

By 1932, the Kelleys had saved enough money to buy a small plot of land in Waikiki. Estelle recollects that they paid $5,000 for the 5,000-foot lot at the corner of Seaside and Kuhio in the heart of Waikiki. Roy designed and supervised the building of the family home on the land.

A 1934 photo in the album shows the young couple holding their first towheaded baby outside of the family home. It is a modest cottage with a small garden.

"We've always had a garden," offered Roy, flashing back to their first one in Hawaii.

They were a handsome family. Roy Kelley, in this picture, has a Gary Cooperish look. Estelle still retains her collegiate winsomeness. The baby Richard is baby cute.

Roy explained how they launched their first commercial real estate development on the same property by building a six-unit apartment house behind the family home. The apartment house was called The Monterey. It cost $10,000 to build.

Today, the corner is the site of the towering Waikiki Trade Center complex. The value of the land is conservatively valued at around $400 a square foot.

"In those days you could borrow up to eighty percent, so I did. I didn't have all that money, that's for sure. In those days we lived from week to week."

"They were cute apartments," recalls Estelle, "and they had HOT water. We rented them for the same amount as the shack we had down at the beach: $45 a month — a bargain!"

The $10,000 cost of the apartments didn't include enough money to install glass in all of the windows, at least not enough to keep rain out during violent rain storms.

"One of our tenants complained that she had to cover herself with an umbrella every time she went to the bathroom,"

Roy laughed.

The Monterey Apartments marked the beginning of the Kelley tradition for providing "clean, comfortable, and affordable accommodations."

Furniture for the apartments was built by local carpenters and hand painted by the Kelleys. Tile for the patios was the same as that used at the Royal Hawaiian Hotel. Roy scavenged broken bits and pieces from the residue found in nearby vacant lots that had been discarded by the Royal's contractor.

"We laid the tile ourselves," says Roy.

With a little help from his friends, his friends recall.

Val Ossipoff, today one of Hawaii's most honored architects, came to Hawaii to work at the C. W. Dickey shop when Roy Kelley was still in charge of the drafting room.

"He ran a good shop. He was very, very important, and he was good. He knew his stuff," Val attests.

"Oh, yes, I remember the Monterey Apartments. Each had an individual entrance from the street through a little patio of about ten by twelve feet. Yes indeed, I helped lay tile in one of those patios from odd sized leftovers from the Royal Hawaiian. It looked nice."

Money was tight and every dollar counted. If the Kelleys could profit from temporary inconvenience, they were willing to be temporarily inconvenienced. If, for example, they found a tenant who was willing to pay $60 a month and there was a rental apartment nearby for $30 a month, the Kelleys would move out and put the difference into a new construction project.

This was nothing new to Estelle. Not only had her mother insisted on having an extra room which she could let out for extra money but her father was a small contractor who would start building the family a home only to sell it before it was finished. He would move the family out and start another house.

Estelle: "Some of the places Roy and I moved into in Waikiki didn't have facilities for cooking so we ate at the

Barbecue Inn next to the Palm Tree Tavern Inn or at a little shack on Kalakaua Avenue near the Moana Hotel.

"This fellow had a counter with a gas burner behind it. He served stew and rice for sixty cents at outdoor tables. That was a good meal for folks like us who had healthy appetites."

In 1933, Richard Kelley was born at Kapiolani Maternity Hospital.

Estelle: "Dr. Garton Wall was the doctor who brought Richard into the world. I knew I didn't want to go to Dr. Milnor, who was one of the founders of the Straub Clinic, because he was a close personal friend of Judge Coke's. I was afraid he would want me to quit work and I wanted to work as long as I could. We needed my salary. That's why I changed over to this other doctor who was going away over the New Year's Holiday, which was all right because Richard was not due until late January. He came on December 28."

Typical Kelley to hasten a project timetable?

"Yep," responds Estelle. "Then it was a Dr. Hodgins who delivered Jean and Pat. I think it was Dr. Hodgins who gave Richard the idea of going into medicine."

In 1933, Roy Kelley, still in the employment of Dickey, received his registration certificate (No. 220) as a professional architect from the Territorial Board of Registration, allowing him to practice independently.

To house his growing family and to have room for his expanding architectural activities, the Kelleys bought another small plot of land across from their apartment house. On the site they built a two-story family home that included a small rentable penthouse. This add-on rental feature was to become a Kelley trademark.

The home also served as an office.

On the ground floor were offices for draftsmen, behind which was a family apartment. A music room and a small penthouse shared the upstairs space.

Dr. Richard Kelley thought hard to bring that early home into focus.

"Yes, I think that house had two floors. We lived in the

The Kelley family pose in their horse and buggy before
the family homestead in Redlands, California. *Circa 1909.*

Chubby little
Roy Kelley stands in
front of his father,
Lewis Franklin Kelley,
mother, Minnie Mae,
half brother, Amos,
half sister, Iva.

Growing up in California. Shots taken in Redlands, San Diego and Los Angeles. Notice the cocked head in the first photo, a Roy Kelley characteristic he will show all of his life.

A boy, above,
enters his teens, left.

Roy Kelley, right, in high school ROTC uniform. "I was bashful then," he said. Below, as a university student at USC, he matures into a handsome collegian.

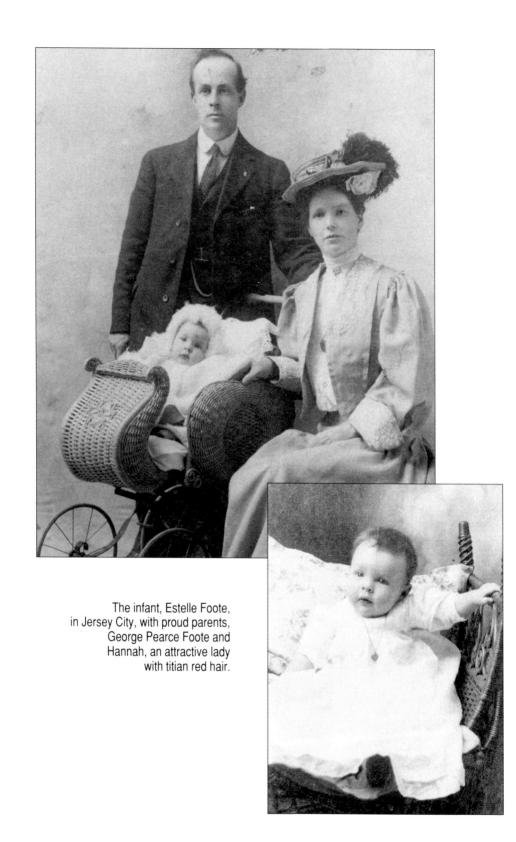

The infant, Estelle Foote,
in Jersey City, with proud parents,
George Pearce Foote and
Hannah, an attractive lady
with titian red hair.

Estelle Foote, right, at age 12, poses with her sister, Doris, age 4.

Estelle in California begins to reflect the inheritance of her mother's beauty.

The outdoor life. Above, at the beach, with Uncle Andrew. Left, hiking in the mountains, where Estelle's father built a vacation cabin.

Estelle Foote's graduation picture from
Los Angeles High School in 1924. She was
not acquainted with another student, a half a
semester ahead of her, named Roy Kelley.

Four years later, still the
same serene and winsome
face of Estelle in her
graduation picture from the
University of California at Los
Angeles in 1928.

Marriage.
Roy Kelley and his
new bride,
Estelle Foote,
at the Church of
the Holy Faith in
Inglewood,
California in May,
1929.

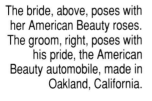

The bride, above, poses with
her American Beauty roses.
The groom, right, poses with
his pride, the American
Beauty automobile, made in
Oakland, California.

Roy and Estelle pose on El Camino Real in front of Mission San Juan Capistrano, California.

Roy and Estelle at the entry to their California home near San Juan Capistrano. Roy personally laid the bricks of the walkway at their feet.

Roy photographs Estelle in front of the couple's first home near San Juan Capistrano, California, where Roy Kelley was the resident architect of the subdivision.

The couple poses in the gazebo Roy Kelley designed as part of the development project. Notice the cocked head again.

Estelle in front of the
$45-a-month cottage in
Dewey Lane where the
Hilton Hawaiian Village
now stands.

The serious young
architect/designer now
with the firm of C.W.
Dickey in Honolulu

The
Territorial Board of Registration
for Professional Engineers
Architects and Surveyors

hereby certifies that

Roy C. Kelley

is duly registered as a professional

Architect

within the Territory of Hawaii

In witness whereof, I have set my hand and caused the Seal of the Territorial Board of Registration for Professional Engineers, Architects and Surveyors to be affixed.

Roy Kelley's
registration
certificate from
the Territory of
Hawaii.

Playtime included beach time. In 1930 Waikiki Beach was fronted with private homes and only two hotels, the Moana and the Royal Hawaiian.

Estelle works on her Hawaiian tan.

The Kelleys went on mountain adventures with their friends. Roy sits in the middle of the waterfall.

Estelle is content to sit demurely at the side of the same waterfall.

In 1934 the first child, Richard, comes into the household. The Kelleys also built their first commercial building, "The Monterey Apartments."

Estelle on shipboard poses with son, Richard. Many years later, her third child, Patricia, is shown as a young lady. The pictures could be of the same woman.

The successful Kelley
couple leave Honolulu
for their first trip to
Europe in 1939.

back and I played in the backyard. I remember guys doing drafting in the front of the house and my mother cooking for all the workmen in the back. She bought rice and sugar in 100-pound bags."

In 1935, the first daughter was born, Jean, and two years later the second daughter, Patricia, joined the family. All the Kelley offspring were born in Kapiolani Maternity Hospital.

In 1936, the couple finished a twenty-unit apartment, the Town House, at Royal Hawaiian Avenue and Kuhio. They didn't have enough money to finish the top floor. A not unusual situation. Roy put a temporary roof over the structure and one day, while he was on the rooftop pondering what he was going to do about it, a sudden strong gust of wind upended the makeshift roof, collapsing it on top of him.

Tommy Perkins, their college chum and architect colleague, was visiting with Estelle down the street. Hearing a big crash, they dashed to the Town House frantically shouting Roy's name. From somewhere under the caved-in roof came a strong but shaky reply: "I'm all right. I'm all right."

"I was all right but I could have been killed," he speaks now from a perspective of a lucky victim. "I was lucky."

Val Ossipoff also remembers the Town House.

"Roy threw a party on the unfinished top floor. We all marveled at an apartment house with three floors in Hawaii. In those days, this was the equivalent of a highrise.

"Things were easier to build in those days. There weren't the strings and regulations and examinations we have today."

By 1938, Roy was doing so much entrepreneurial work out of his makeshift office in his Waikiki home that he left Dickey.

In adulthood, Richard once asked his father why he made the transition out of Dickey's office. "'You know,' he told me, 'I was embarrassed because I was spending so much time working on other people's projects.'"

The Kelleys accumulated property in Waikiki as a way of life. The chronological history of the acquisitions, their locations and prices have never been publicly disclosed but there has been a lot of speculation about the Kelleys' real estate holdings. According to one newspaper account, they were, reputedly, the owners of forty-three parcels of Waikiki property. People who knew the Waikiki real estate scene at the time say that figure was probably too low.

Empty lots that once held Royal Hawaiian Hotel building refuse, the source of the Kelleys' paving tile for their first apartment house, were among those picked up by the far-sighted young architect and his supportive wife.

After the break from the Dickey firm and with a strong load of design work for solely-owned and in-partnership apartments, the Kelleys reached an early stage of financial independence.

That same year, the couple made their first trip to Europe.

"We worked seven days a week from the very beginning. But when the time came to take a vacation, we took it," Estelle said.

Friends advised against their going to Europe because of the threatening international situation.

Hitler had taken over Austria and Czechoslovakia and although Neville Chamberlain returned from a summit meeting with Hitler waving a piece of paper and saying it represented "peace in our time," the clouds of war were gathering.

Roy: "A taxi driver in New York taking us down to the pier to catch the boat held up a newspaper with the headline, 'WAR IN 24 HOURS.' Didn't slow us down. We just got on the ship and went. Going back to the Old Country and looking at the classic buildings is a thing an architect has to do."

London was already getting ready for war. Sand bags were being placed around buildings. People were carrying gas masks.

Estelle, on their visit to Westminster Abbey, reflects, "A guide led us through the abbey, telling us about the history. With the statues all around and the light coming through the stained glass windows, it was the most beautiful thing I ever saw." She paused. Then offhandedly: "The Archbishop of Canterbury is a good friend of ours. He stays in our hotel when he comes. Very nice chap."

Roy: "In Paris there was no sign that a war was coming on. Our hotel was very close to one of the big avenues. I noticed the taxis waiting in front of it all the time. So I went down and asked one of the taxi drivers how much would it cost for him to drive us down to Rome. He told me and I said, 'We leave tomorrow morning.'

"I remember in Italy we were in a grotto someplace sightseeing and this little old Italian lady came up and asked me if I had any children. I said yes and she wanted to know how many and I said, 'Three.'

"And she said, 'Mussolini would be very proud of you.'"

After enjoying the sights of Rome, particularly the estate gardens such as the Villa d'Este, the couple sailed for home from Naples.

The Prewar Period—1938 to 1941

Life for the Kelleys was not all work. They established a Sunday morning custom of entertaining at breakfast, starring Estelle's homemade waffles.

They attended professional socials. A photo in the scrapbook shows a line-up of architects at a costume dance party at Waialae Country Club. "Biggest bunch of rascals on earth," Roy laughs fondly at the picture. "We had a lot of fun."

The Kelleys joined Oahu Country Club where Estelle proved to be a strong golfer.

They were also avid bridge players. One friend remembers that the holder of the 'dummy' hand would lie down on the floor and get a massage from the Kelleys' Japanese maid.

Roy Kelley's hobby was painting, particularly with water colors.

Both enjoyed travel, when and as time permitted.

Turn another page in the family album and there is a

family picture aboard ship. Roy, Estelle and the three children on their way to California in 1940.

Over the years the parents took the children on three trips to Europe, one to Africa, several to tour the United States. They spent time on dude ranches, toured Colonial Williamsburg and took in the sights of New York.

On one trip to the Mainland, the family visited the hotel school at Cornell and Jeannie resolved to get her degree there.

"Our trips usually meant that our parents couldn't be reached. They wouldn't take telephone calls. When we would go to a dude ranch, for example, they wouldn't go riding or take part in any of the activities, but would be content to stay in their cabin and read, recharging their batteries." Jeannie remembers.

One time, it was said, Roy and Estelle made a trip around the world without ever having an advance hotel reservation.

Flipping a few family photo album pages forward, one sees the family members at their Diamond Head home.

Here is a head shot of Patricia as an attractive young adult. She looks so much like her mother that it is difficult to believe she is not the same woman featured prominently in the earlier pages of the album.

Today Pat is the most vivacious of the three children. She exudes energy. Conversation flows out of her with artesian well ease. She has grown a bit matronly and wears spectacles but still reflects the attractive spirit and rebel reputation she always held within the family.

Another picture shows a skinny, shy Jeannie holding a surveyor's measuring rod. She is perhaps six years old.

Jeannie is carrot haired — like her brother — an inheritance from Estelle's mother. Slim, trim, attractive and precise, she hikes, canoes, takes exotic international tours and bangs a tennis forehand cross court like a professional.

Richard is Dr. Kelley to his employees, Richard to his family and Rich to his old school pals. He still wears about him an air of medical sobriety and his keen gaze through metal rimmed glasses is of a physician examining a medical problem. He is low key, soft spoken. While not as volatile as his father, he has inherited Roy's brilliance and some of his mannerisms. "Here,' he says, pulling out a pad, "I'll draw you a picture."

When and how did the Kelleys move from a workshop home on Kuhio Avenue to an oceanfront, two-story estate house on Diamond Head, one of the most desirable residential locations in Honolulu?

One of Roy's clients was a Dr. Fred Alsup, a prominent physician who founded the Alsup Clinic. The doctor had a home on Diamond Head. During the course of designing a new driveway for Dr. Alsup's property, Roy mentioned that he would be interested in buying the home if the doctor ever wanted to sell it.

Richard contends that "Fred Alsup was very smart, very worldly. He had a feeling that war was imminent and began to liquidate all of his assets."

One night, late in 1941, Val Ossipoff, the architect, and his wife were at the Kelleys for dinner when Roy received a telephone call from Dr. Alsup asking if he were still interested in the Diamond Head house. It was for sale.

Roy grabbed Estelle, left the dinner guests to finish for themselves, drove out to Diamond Head and concluded a deal with the good doctor.

"It was a lovely piece of land. We paid $45,000 for it, $5,000 down and the rest was carried by the doctor," recalls Roy.

The family didn't move into the home formally for almost five years.

The purchase of the Diamond Head home was made just before December 7, 1941, the day the Japanese attacked Pearl Harbor.

The memory of that day endures in the minds of all members of the Kelley family.

Mounted in the family album are clippings of Pearl Harbor anniversaries. The reliving of those days brings tears to

Roy Kelley's eyes.

"I can't help it," he says, turning away from the album and blotting his face with a handkerchief.

Jeannie remembers, as they were driving off to St. Clement's Episcopal Church to Sunday School, that the sky was full of dark explosions. The family thought it was still another military exercise.

Not until later in the morning did the Pearl Harbor news reach the Kelley household. Roy drove frantically back to get his children.

Pat recalls the scene with her father: "He came screaming into the church telling everybody to go home. Pearl Harbor was being attacked. As we drove by this building at King Street and McCully, it was hit by an anti-aircraft shell and burst into flames. We drove another block and a half and a building to our right, near the Japanese school, got it.

"We got into Waikiki and at the intersection of Lewers and Kuhio, the car stalled. Well, we got it going again and, as we drove off, we heard a tremendous explosion behind us. There, where our car had stalled, was a great big gaping hole where an anti-aircraft shell had exploded.

"On the same corner was an apartment building that father had designed for Harry Good. He owned Harry Good's Liquors in Waikiki. Harry and his wife, Carmen, were bridge playing pals of my parents. In one of those corner apartments a tenant bent over to listen more closely to the news on the radio just as a piece of shrapnel from the same explosion went right over her head and left a hole in the wall. If she had been standing up she would have been beheaded."

"He brought the kids home and dropped them on my lap," remembers Estelle. "He was worried about an apartment building we had at the corner of Royal Hawaiian Avenue and Kuhio. We thought a bomb had dropped on it.

"We had a naval officer from the *USS Oklahoma* as a tenant. He was on duty aboard the ship and was relieved by a fellow officer and went below to get some rest when the ship was hit. His fellow officer was blown off the ship and was saved, but our tenant was trapped below deck and went down with the ship."

The family moved into the basement of their first apartment.

"That basement had a large storage room where we normally stored steamer trunks in racks built into the walls," Estelle continued.

"We had just received a shipment of springs and mattresses so we cleared out the trunks, opened up the springs and mattresses, popped them into the trunk racks and we had perfect bunks. We were set."

Pat remembers how the family Sunday morning tradition of Mom's waffles continued, uninterrupted. Roy sent the maid across the street to get the waffle iron. She didn't want to go. Roy raised his voice to her and, in fear of him, she got halfway across, panicked and ran back again. Roy raised his voice another notch — she was more afraid of him than the Japanese! — so she finally got the waffle iron and the family had Sunday waffles.

"I remember mother tucking us into bed, Jeannie and I in different mattresses. That's the night I learned the Lord's Prayer. Up until then my father would come to my bed and he'd say, 'Now I lay me down to sleep, I pray the Lord my soul to keep' and then he'd tell me about the angel that slept on top of my bed to protect me.

"But that Sunday, December 7th of 1941, my mother taught me the Lord's Prayer. I learned it all in one night and I have said it every night since. It was a very traumatic time for all of us."

Richard's version of the day parallels Pat's.

"I remember being dropped off at Sunday school. My father had guests for breakfast. They often had sort of a Sunday morning breakfast party when my mother would make waffles. That was a big part of their lives. They were having waffles with a navy captain.

"I remember walking up to the teacher because there was hardly anybody there. I said, 'Where is everybody?'

"And she said, 'Don't you know there is a war on?'

"And I said, in effect, 'What's a war?'

"My father came and picked us up. I remember we went to the top floor of our building and I have this vision of a big black cloud of black smoke out there, and seeing planes diving in and out. Then we heard a high pitched whine and the corner of Kuhio and Lewers sort of erupted. That's when we made a beeline for the cellars across the street.

"Another memory I have is of somebody bringing in a piece of shrapnel and it was still hot.

Jeannie has her own distinct memories. "On the way to Sunday school that morning there were these little black puffy clouds over Punchbowl. I can still see those clouds today.

"I remember my father racing into the classroom and grabbing me and throwing me in the back of the car, and I was so upset because I hadn't finished coloring my picture for the day in Sunday School.

"My parents were in the middle of breakfast having Sunday morning waffles with a captain of a ship in Pearl Harbor when they got the news. I think his ship left him because it had to get out of the harbor.

"We moved into the cellar of the apartments across the street. That was the year my father was giving Richard an electric train set for Christmas. In the room next to us he had set up the train on a big green board with tracks and all. I remember looking through the crack at night and seeing the train in there and not letting Richard see because it was for his Christmas."

Richard: "I remember coming out at night and looking up at the sky and it was just full of tracers. Evidently, some of our planes were en route to Honolulu and by the time they arrived after the Japanese attack, everybody thought they were enemies and the military tried to shoot them down."

(Six carrier airplanes from the *USS Enterprise* which was two hundred miles at sea during the attack were sent to Ford Island in Pearl Harbor as reinforcements. Four were shot down by trigger-happy anti-aircraft batteries.)

Pat: "We eventually moved out to the house on Diamond Head. No furniture. Just mattresses on the floor. Black out curtains all over. Barbed wire fencing all over the front yard facing the ocean.

"We had no civil law," Pat went on. "We had military law. You could get court martialed for speeding. You could get shot for having a light on at night. Civil law went out the window. They locked up locally born Japanese under any pretext.

"They came along and said, 'You, Roy Kelley. You are essential to the war effort. Go out to Pearl Harbor and start building. To the rest of the family they said, 'You are in the way here. Go back to California where you have family.'

"Before that we were all finger printed and made to carry identification cards. We were issued gas masks. They took all our money away from us. Issued us receipts until we got money that had 'Hawaii' printed on it. Punahou campus was taken over by the military.

"So it was decided that we should be evacuated and go to California for the duration of the war."

Estelle and the three children, along with one Ossipoff infant, gained passage on a Pan American Clipper departing from Honolulu to Oakland. For the children it was an eye-opening, frightening, eighteen-hour flying experience.

It took three attempts at takeoff before the amphibian aircraft lumbered out of the waters of Keehi Lagoon.

Jeannie: "We were all cramped together on the plane. There was a hard table with seats facing each other. The table didn't collapse and couldn't be stored away. I remember sleeping on the floor of the plane under the table."

For Roy Kelley, it was traumatic. He cried for fear he would never would see his family again.

Estelle reminisces: "The plan was for us to go to my parents in Los Angeles. We got seats on the Clipper and flew to the Bay Area with one of the Ossipoff children who we were supposed to give to Mrs. Ossipoff's sister in San Francisco. When we landed in Oakland, we were taken to Treasure Island and interrogated by the FBI. Here I was: Kelley, Kelley, Kelley, Kelley and Ossipoff. I'll never forget it.

"We then took the South Pacific Daylight from Oakland to Los Angeles."

For Roy the worst news was yet to come.

"The Navy put a notice in the paper that they wanted architects and engineers to volunteer. So I went down and volunteered. The time came for my physical exam. It took about two hours and when it was all finished and the doctor was casually picking things up, he said, 'You do know that you'll be blind within six months, don't you?'

"It was the first time I had any idea that I had an eye problem. I was already by myself. In those days they didn't know much about cataracts. I still had my apartments to run."

It was obvious to Roy Kelley that he was going to need help and that he, too, would have to go to the Mainland.

"When the time came for me to leave, I turned the apartments over to a tenant of ours. He was the retired head of Sears, Roebuck. A wonderful man. I had total trust in him. So I left everything to him to manage. He did a good job.

"At that stage I could still see well enough to get on a boat for California, and then to Los Angeles on the train. I called Mama from the station where I got off and she came and got me. I could still see but my vision was getting dim by that time."

The couple first moved in with her parents and then bought a little bungalow in Fox Hills near the Fox motion picture sound stages.

One morning at breakfast, Roy Kelley, the gifted architect, suddenly went blind. Completely blind.

Here he was, a professional whose livelihood depended on his sight, suddenly sightless.

When asked five decades later what effect it had on him, he replies good heartedly, "Well, by that time I had enough money so I didn't have to worry."

Then, typically, he breaks into song: "*Que Sera, Sera, Sera —.*"

What will be will be, will be.

CHAPTER THREE

California ...
The Long Voyage Home ...
The First Hotels

Despite Roy Kelley's brave front, it had to be a precarious time. A blind architect in a strange house, in a city he no longer knew. The family's assets tied up in real estate in a war zone.

W̲ho was going to win the war?
Would the Japanese try to take the Islands?
What was going to happen to Hawaii?
Nobody knew.
How were they going to get funds out of the Territory?
Even that wasn't sure.
What was he going to do with his life?
He couldn't have known.
The immediate task was to take care of Roy Kelley. Estelle remembers, "The kids were very patient with their father. They walked blocks and blocks with him every day. Waited for signals to cross streets. Watched out for curbs, trees, hydrants."

Pat speculates about how hard it must have been on Estelle. "Mother suddenly had a blind person to take care of, a house that had to have furniture placed where Daddy wouldn't run into it, food that had to be just so on the plate so he could find it, and three bratty children — all under eight — running around under foot.

"Were we good little children? No. We fought like hell. All three of us. We were raised to be independent, to think as individuals, so we were naturally headstrong. Independent, hard-to-control children.

"You have to understand that Jeannie was mother's pet. She was sensitive. I was Daddy's pet, and Richard was always Prince Charming, 'The Anointed One,' to both of them.

"In those days I was a seeing-eye dog for my father. Mother used to push us out of the house so she could clean it, and I would walk Daddy around the neighborhood while Jeannie and Richard were in school. He taught me to see color. I could not just tell him that the trees were green. I had to tell him exactly what shades of green. I had to speak to him very clearly in colors you use when you paint. He taught me how to paint while he was totally blind.

"I became Daddy's best friend in a lot of ways. He raised me as a boy. He didn't think of me as a girl.

"I was not an easy child. I was wild. I was rambunctious. I was spoiled. But I was always Daddy's Girl. I was the only one of us allowed in his office. I can remember Daddy drafting while I played under the drafting table.

"Jeannie is much more proper. I always think of her as 'The Lady.' She is my grandmother and my mother incarnate. She is a wonderful person, has tremendous character. My father never saw my sister as a human being because she was a 'girl.' He was the original male chauvinist. Archie Bunker's Archie Bunker.

"Why did he give mother so much authority when she was a woman? I often asked Daddy that, and he would just say that she was different. He had his own exception to the rules. Estelle was one; I was another.

"I have to say that my mother was a perfect partner for him. I don't think he would have made it if it hadn't been for Estelle being here to kind of smooth over the rough edges.

When father went out and cut a path through the jungle, he didn't always pay much attention to where he was cutting, or if the time was right to cut. Mother was the diplomat who followed through ... covering things up."

R̲oy was accepted at Mayo Clinic in Rochester for eye surgery.

On the way to Rochester, the couple had to overnight in Chicago because they couldn't make transportation connections. It was the middle of the war; there wasn't a room to be had. Standing forlornly in the lobby of the Palmer House, they were approached by the manager who, seeing the blind man being led by a lady, wondered if they had a problem.

Estelle told him that they couldn't find a room. They only needed it for one night. The manager took care of them.

"It was only a broom closet but we were so grateful," says Estelle. As she looked back to that dismal event, her shoulders involuntarily slumped. But the day has never been forgotten.

It has been remembered, in fact, in the most effective manner. In the history of Kelley innkeeping, there has been a constant, unpublicized, forty-year tradition of taking care of those in need of shelter.

F̲ollowing the operation at the Mayo Clinic, Roy Kelley's eyes were bandaged shut, his head immobilized.

Jeannie: "In those days cataract patients had to stay in the hospital for a month, completely blacked out, sand bags around their head. No movement was permitted. I remember them saying, because the sand bags pressed so hard around his head, that his ears looked like cauliflowers."

When the bandages were removed, sight had been partially restored in the right eye but the left eye was not corrected. Shortly after leaving the hospital the retina in the bad eye became detached and hope for eventual sight in the eye was lost forever.

The Long Voyage Home

As soon as Roy felt well enough to travel, he applied for passage to Honolulu. He returned in 1943.

What did he bring back in his luggage?

A flush toilet.

Roy: "It was simple logic. There wasn't any room in Hawaii. If I threw somebody out of one of my apartments, he wouldn't be able to find anything and I would be out of the rent money but, if I had a toilet, I could hook it up somewhere and I'd have a room. Well, I had a little construction shack next to one of my properties so, as soon as I arrived back in Honolulu, I installed the toilet. And I had a place to stay.

"I was involved in taking back the management of our properties. There was no architectural work at that time. Construction was at a standstill. You couldn't get permission to build anything or to change anything.

"Fortunately, I had pre-war permits to build on the Seaside Avenue property in the same area where our first home had been built. We added a few modest cottages."

Roy's biggest challenge, however, was to get the family back home.

The Pacific war, by 1944, had retreated from the shores of Hawaii and the family applied for permission to return from California.

Pat recalls the voyage home. "It took us five days to get out of San Francisco Harbor and, instead of the normal five days to make the crossing, it took ten days. We zigzagged back and forth across huge expanses of ocean in convoy to avoid detection before we reached Rabbit Island off the Oahu shore in the Molokai Channel.

"I have a very vivid memory of the time because we could smell Hawaii. We could smell the flowers across the water. It was so, so very close, so tempting. We steamed back and forth for a full day before we could finally get into the harbor. Daddy moved us into the big house on Diamond Head."

Jeannie remembers the ship as being a hospital ship.

"We had triple bunks. Everybody was violently seasick. We had these horrible lifejackets that stained the clothes and smelled terrible and you had to wear them all the time. The food was terrible, but we couldn't eat anyway ... didn't want to eat."

"About the time the family came back," Roy remembers, "I got a call from Kingie Kimball."

The Kimball family owned and managed the Halekulani Hotel.

"I had done the design for the central core building of the Halekulani — the only part of the original structure that still remains. I thought he wanted to talk about more design work."

Kingie Kimball remembers the call very well. He tells the story, "It was right near the end of the war. I got a call from Allan Moore of the Hawaiian Trust Company which controlled the trust of the Alton J. Cohen Estate.

"The estate owned the Edgewater Apartments which were built on three beach lots between my Halekulani Hotel and the YWCA beach house next to Fort DeRussy.

"Each lot covered 50,000 square feet. There was a total of 150,000 square feet for sale at a price of $325,000. He wanted to know if my family was interested in buying the property.

"We were pretty well committed so I said no, I didn't think so. Then he asked if I knew anybody who would be interested in the lots. I told him to give me a couple of days to think about it.

"Right away I called Roy Kelley and told him to come down and see me, that I had something I wanted him to look at.

"He wanted to know what it was but I just said to come down and I would show him.

"Well, he drove down from wherever he worked near Kuhio and I met him on the sidewalk by my hotel.

"I walked him over to the Edgewater Apartments. They were nice apartments. You could drive down into the property. I told him that they were for sale.

"As we got into the area, he kept walking faster and

faster and he got more and more excited until he was ahead of me, leaving me behind. He walked down to the beach and walked back as fast as he could, passing me on the way back, and saying, 'I've got to show this to Estelle.'

"He got into his car and zoomed up Lewers Road and that was the last I saw of him until a couple of days later. I asked him if he had made any move towards buying the Edgewater Apartments.

"'Oh,' he said, 'I went down the next day and gave Hawaiian Trust a certified check for $60,000 to hold the property. By the way,' he added, 'thank you very much.'"

One reason the Cohen Estate wanted to sell the apartments was because the firing of the 14-inch naval guns from Battery Randolph in the adjacent Fort DeRussy had severely damaged some of the apartments in the two-story wooden building.

When the powerful fourteen-inch naval guns of Battery Randolph with a fourteen-mile range were test fired in peace, they shook the buildings in downtown Honolulu so violently that there was a volatile public outcry against them. The guns were seldom fired thereafter.

The result of the firings numbed the apartments next door. Richard Kelley's recollection of the Edgewater Apartments is one of dilapidation, cracked walls and loose light bulbs suspended from the ceiling.

His father patched up the apartments and put them out for rent.

"Yes, I went right downtown and bought the property," Roy confirms. "I forget the price but I remember that I stipulated in the contract that, if there were any reparations for damages caused by the coastal guns, the money would revert to me. I later collected $15,000 in damages.

"The Edgewater Apartments was one of many examples of opportunities being pushed in front of me that I grabbed. I was just lucky."

Hold on. Kingie Kimball reported that Roy Kelley "got in his car and drove up Lewers Road," didn't he? How could a man almost blind drive a car?

It didn't last long.

Roy Kelley recalls the day.

"I gave up driving on the corner of Royal Hawaiian and Kuhio. I was going down Kuhio and this sonofabitch thought he'd beat me to the intersection. Well, he didn't have a chance of beating me to the intersection because he was on my blind side and I didn't know he was there. I was only going about twenty-five miles an hour but I sure knocked him to hell. Nobody was hurt and he never did sue me. I don't know why he didn't sue me. After that, I gave up driving. I could have been killed."

After the war ended, building controls eased, permitting Kelley to resume construction on his property around the Seaside/Kuhio corner. More cottages were built as rentals, often in financial partnerships with friends.

"Those were good times, lots of fun," Roy will tell his listener.

"We got building materials all right. It was a funny period because, technically, we couldn't get material. But the government never did follow through on technical things."

His labor came from manual arts students at Kamehameha School — they got practical experience in carpentry and credit for their courses — and from moonlighting Seabees from the Navy who sought extra money to spend on Hotel Street.

So much of the property behind the Waikiki Theater was dominated by Kelley cottages that the narrow access lane to the back cottages was dubbed "Kelley's Alley."

The First Hotel

During the initial development of the cottages in 1943 — and because he had held a building permit allowing it — Roy had laid the foundation for a large building.

Roy: "So with a valid building permit and the foundation already there, I was able to go ahead and build this little hotel — our first."

The hotel was called The Islander. The year was 1947. The hotel is gone now and its site is occupied by Waikiki Theaters #1 and #2.

"It was a four-story walkup with thirty-three rooms. Actually, there were five stories because, on top, we added a small penthouse. We always tried to include a penthouse. Actually, at The Islander we didn't have enough money to complete the penthouse so we just put a roof over the top floor and left it until we could afford to finish it.

"Most of the downstairs rooms rented for $7.50 a day, but the penthouse would bring $10 a day." (The penthouse included two bedrooms, one bath, a living room and kitchen.)

The Islander was the first hotel built in Hawaii for people unable to pay the prices asked by the Royal Hawaiian, the Moana, and the Halekulani hotels.

Low cost hotel rooms demanding high occupancy percentages was a Kelley format for the next forty years. It was a niche in the market place that the Kelleys dominated and on which they built their pyramiding successes.

Press Roy for the secret of his success and he may take two seconds and push papers around on the table in front of him or rotate his head in gentle jerks, pondering the question, but his answer most probably will be a quick single word: "Luck!" For emphasis, he will slam his hand down on the table top, tilt his head backwards and explode with laughter.

Indeed, the second major sequence of Kelley hotel development could not have been foreseen.

"The events leading to the building of our second hotel, the Edgewater Hotel, was another typical example of practically everything I have done. Good things were just pushed in front of me," Roy Kelley insists.

He takes you back to a sunny morning in the mid-Forties.

"I was mowing the lawn at my little building on Seaside and this lady drove up to the curb, parked her car and came over to me. She said she was the owner of property at Beachwalk and Kalia Road across the street from my Edgewater Apartments, and she wanted to sell it.

"We drove over to her place — it was called the Willard Inn — and we closed the deal in a matter of minutes.

"We always buy everything in one day. We don't fool around.

"Ninety percent of the properties I bought were properties I had no intention of buying. Hadn't even given thought to them. People walked up and said, 'I want to sell to you.' Worked out very well. All my life.

"We didn't buy the Willard Inn at that time; just took it over on a lease basis. Later, after she died, the two sons wanted to get out of it and offered to sell the land to me at fee simple which meant I would own the property outright. I paid $2 million for it around 1949.

"The property was two-hundred-feet square ...just about one acre. There were about twenty units in the Willard Inn."

Shortly after its purchase, Kelley made plans to build the second Kelley hotel, the Edgewater Hotel. Construction began on the one-acre site of a hundred-room, six-floor building that incorporated revolutionary features: the first automatic elevator in Hawaii, and — wonder of wonders — a swimming pool.

People thought Roy Kelley was crazy. Why have a swimming pool when you were only two hundred feet from the ocean?

But the most revolutionary feature was the room price structure. For the first time in Hawaii, visitors had a new hotel room almost on the beach, at a modest rate. The philosophy established at the Monterey Apartments and extended to The Islander Hotel of providing clean, comfortable rooms at affordable rates was carried over to the Edgewater.

The same people who told Kelley that he was crazy to build a hotel with a swimming pool later told him he was crazy to charge such low room rates.

The Edgewater was sold out from the day it opened.

Although the little Islander was a hotel, it was the hundred-room Edgewater that sparked the evolution of the

Kelley clan from rental entrepreneurs to innkeepers.

Without any hotel training, Roy Kelley instinctively knew that the duty post of a professional innkeeper was the lobby, the core of the operation.

He worked directly with guests. He would carry baggage if there was no one else available. (And keep the tip, although he denies it today.) He'd go into the basement and get toilet paper. Answer the phone. Take reservations. Whatever was needed.

If Roy couldn't do it, Estelle would.

Roy's desk was established right by the front desk, which became another Kelley trademark. It facilitated his own peculiar brand of "rooms control."

If a person had only $5 and Roy Kelley had an empty room, that person had a $5 room. If it were a family, Roy would find them larger quarters. If they were Canadians, Roy would find a unit with a kitchen. "Canadians like to do their own cooking."

It was those early days that established his reputation for dealing his cash in and out of a cigar box. When he accumulated enough cash in the cigar box, he invested in another construction project.

Early Recruits

In the days after the war, two enduring employees joined the Kelleys.

"At the Willard Inn," Roy remembers, 'There was a little girl working for the hotel who served hot coffee to each of the guests in the morning. Her name was Peggy Hatori. She later became a cashier. A very, very thorough girl. She stills works for us.

"Ruth Harada is another. An architect downtown called me and said he was going to close down because of the lack of work and he had a secretary he thought I could use. So I said, 'Send her out.'"

Ruth Harada, ageless, is still Roy Kelley's secretary.

Early employees, honor graduates of the "Kelley Hotel

School," remember the first days of the Edgewater Hotel with fondness.

Lyman Blank had just graduated from the Cornell University Hotel School when he met a director of the Hawaii Visitors Bureau who was passing through Ithaca on his way to New York City.

He gave Lyman several names to contact in Hawaii, including that of Roy Kelley. Lyman wrote each person asking for a job. Kelley's manager of the Edgewater wrote back and said there was a job open as catering manager at the Edgewater.

Lyman got the job at a salary of $400 a month, room and board included, and reimbursement for his airfare to Hawaii, provided he stayed six months in the job.

"It was very generous," Lyman says of the terms. "It was probably the top salary of my class. True. My colleagues were going to Sheratons and Hiltons for $250 and $300 a month, without room and board.

"Dick Edwards, the manager, met me at the airport and I started that same day. I must have met Roy very soon afterwards because he was never far away from the front desk.

"The Kelley family went away that summer in spite of a union contract that was being negotiated with Art Rutledge.

"At that time, Bob and Emmie MacGregor had a little table off the lobby where they sold various sightseeing tours to the pineapple fields and the Dole Cannery to watch the packers, or to the neighbor islands — that kind of thing. That was the beginning of Trade Wind Tours which grew into a multi-million dollar operation.

"Roy had an expression he used, to train us to his kind of thoroughness. 'Did you see the body?' In other words, if you were making a decision, did you touch all the elements, feel them, kick them? Did you see the body?

"Another characteristic was his habit of always having pads of paper wherever he was. He had such a brilliant mind that he would become exasperated when people didn't understand him and he would whip out a pad of paper and draw a diagram. Usually it would start with a straight line down the center of the pad and he would say, pointing, 'Now here are the mountains and here is the ocean. You got that?'

"Boy, when that paper came out, you knew you were in trouble. He would draw simple pictures, very simple, and say, 'Now, you see this? Now, you do this.'

"Roy Kelley kept everything in his head. He had spare parts, odd bits of furniture, pieces of lumber were stored all over Waikiki. At the old Islander Hotel. Down in apartment basements. On empty lots. On different pieces of property. He knew where everything was, but it was all in his head.

"He had a bookkeeper, a very accomplished accountant, but Roy used to drive him nuts. The accountant would keep trying to piece things together for a report so there would be something respectable for the Internal Revenue Service, but Roy would have all the numbers in his head. Amazing man.

"One day I was walking with him through the Edgewater addition which was going up right behind the first building. Legally, remember, he was half blind. He stopped once and looked back at a door frame and said, 'That's out of alignment.' Out came the pad and he wrote himself a note, and the next thing you knew there was a carpenter up there putting that door frame in correctly.

"Once, at a Hawaii Hotel Association meeting on a neighbor island he bet me a dollar that Chuck Rolles, his son-in-law, and Richard Kelley would beat Harry Meyer and me in a golf match. Well, he lost and paid off. We had everybody autograph the dollar bill. I had it framed with a caption that read 'The Only Dollar Roy Kelley Lost in His Whole Life.' I gave it to him on his seventy-fifth birthday. He got a big kick out of it."

The nature of Roy Kelley would never let him stand still for success. As soon as the Edgewater enjoyed full occupancy he moved into building an addition next door. A) He had the cash. B) He had the plans. The size was to be the same, one hundred rooms, but this time, instead of hiring a private contractor, he would be his own contractor.

By 1952, the second building was underway. At the

same time, Roy had an option on a property across from the Royal Hawaiian Hotel on Kalakaua, where the International Market Place now stands.

He was also elected president of the Hawaii Hotel Association.

From the beginning, Estelle Kelley was a full partner in the family business.

One supplier in the early days said, "I used to go by Estelle's little office in the Edgewater and she would be very courteous and say, 'Come in and sit down.' Always had time for a little chat. And Roy would always be nearby. I never saw again a couple who paid such close attention to business. They made a fantastic team, the way they worked together."

During the apartment building days, Estelle supervised the registration of occupants, oversaw the cleaning, and collected the rents.

With the opening of the Edgewater, she took over reservations, devising her own system for control. Individual bookings were written on yellow slips of paper and pinioned on a two-spindle board.

"When the yellow pile reached three fingers in height, I knew I had to cut off reservations," the former legal secretary noted.

"I was always kind of leery of what Roy had in his hip pocket, knowing he'd take a reservation and forget to tell me."

No request for information or space was allowed to go unanswered for more than twenty-four hours and the answering letters were typed out on an old fashioned, manual typewriter.

Estelle Kelley operated her home grown system until she retired twenty years later.

The "Estelle Method" was replaced by a computer and six operators!

In 1989, a new Outrigger computer system, a $1.5 million operation capable of servicing a hundred hotels, was named, appropriately, the STELLEX SYSTEM.

During summer college breaks Richard brought home classmates who either worked at one of the Kelley hotels or played beach boy. It became a family custom.

"Friends I brought home went on to become surgeons and lawyers and successful professional men. I still hear from them and they all remember their summers in Hawaii as highlights of their lives."

One summer he brought home his girl friend, Jane Zieber, whom he later married.

Jeannie brought home Chuck Rolles from Cornell, and later married him.

Pat took a short cut and brought home husbands.

"She's had five, you know," says Estelle laconically.

In the summer of 1952 Richard and his Stanford classmate Bob Berglund were working at the Edgewater. As was the family custom, parents and kids assembled at five in the lobby to drive home to Diamond Head for the family evening meal.

Richard was driving the first car with his father seated in front and Bob in back. Estelle followed in a second car.

On Diamond Head where the road comes down towards Waikiki in a sweeping curve, an inebriated sailor missed the turn and smashed into the lead Kelley car.

"All I can remember," recalls Richard, "is seeing three streaks of light coming toward me. The streaks must have been reflections from chrome strippings on the side of the sailor's car. He had gone across the highway into the wall and was coming back into the road when he hit us. It wasn't straight on, or we would all have been killed."

Richard was thrown out onto the pavement. His mother arrived on the scene to see her son lying absolutely motionless in the middle of the road. She thought he was dead.

Roy was still pinned in the car. It took a quarter of an hour to extricate him from the wreckage.

Remembers Roy: "I told the man who was moving me to be careful because my leg was through the floor of the car. Actually, what had happened was the leg was so badly smashed that it was all bundled up under me. It's funny when you have an accident like that. You have no pain. I never had a bit of pain. The next day in the hospital some good friends were talking to me and I started to laugh and, my God, I nearly keeled over with pain. It was unbelievable."

Richard's head had hit the steering wheel and his nose was spread all over his face. He was conscious by the time his mother reached him and convinced her that he was all right.

Roy's scalp was laid back from his head and the scar still shows.

"I told you we were lucky. You can't believe the luck we have had."

From that day on Roy would never walk without a cane.

Naturally, he left the hospital early.

He rented a special hospital bed and converted one of the rooms under construction in the Edgewater addition into his own private hospital ward, with private nurses. From there, he supervised the building of the new hotel wing.

Richard: "I can still see him being wheeled down halls engulfed by plaster, laths and construction debris, barking orders at surprised workmen.

Another room was furnished for Jeannie, adjacent to Roy Kelley's Recovery Room.

Jeannie: "One night when I was getting ready for bed, I looked down through the louvers to the hallway and there was a pair of eyes staring at me. A Peeping Tom! I scooted out to the lanai and around to Mommy and Daddy's room and screamed 'There's a man outside of my door.' With that, Daddy bolted out of his wheelchair and — practically naked — rushed out of the room and down the hall brandishing his cane, swearing to kill the 'sonofabitch.'

"It's now one of the family legends."

P art of Roy's healing process was to clean the hotel swimming pool. Natural water therapy, he called it.

"It helped. There was a local bank vice president who had been down in Texas somewhere and he had a head-on collision. He was all broken up and was back here recuperating. He saw me moving around in the water and it was obvious I was getting better so he joined me every day in cleaning the swimming pool. The hotel owner and the bank officer: pool cleaners. That pool was never that clean before, or since."

As outgoing president of the Hawaii Hotel Association, Roy addressed the sixth annual convention via radiophone from his makeshift hospital bed.

In his farewell address, he reported that the association had established a permanent office with a paid secretary, the year had set new records for visitor arrivals and the industry was already suffering a room shortage.

He warned his fellow members against overcharging for accommodations, encouraged them to keep alive the Aloha Spirit, and urged their support of the fledgling Hawaii Visitors Bureau.

Before his 1952 auto accident, Roy Kelley had an option on the land occupied later by the International Market Place. He wanted to create an exotic assortment of shops and entertainment spots using a famous Shanghai name of "Bubbling Well Road" and connecting Kalakaua Avenue with Kuhio Avenue. The option was passed over after the accident.

The first objective was to finish the new wing of the Edgewater Hotel.

With the completion of the addition, the Edgewater Hotel had two hundred rooms.

Across the street, where the dilapidated Edgewater Apartments stood, the temptation to build on the perfectly beautiful beach was irresistible

It was not too long before construction action started on the oceanfront property. The name of the new project was the Reef Hotel.

There were financial difficulties.

Roy: "Nice man staying at the Halekulani Hotel next door to the Reef while it was under construction used to come by and visit. By this time, the cigar box was getting rather empty.

It was obvious that I was going to need help in finishing the first phase of the new hotel. About a million dollars of help.

"In the course of our conversation I told the visitor about my economic problems and this man said, 'Wait 'til I get back to Minneapolis and I'll call some friends in Texas. I'll get you the million dollars.' And he did."

A 1954 newspaper article describes Roy Kelley arriving at the building site at seven a.m. seven days a week to supervise workers pouring concrete, plastering, hammering and sawing. Out front they are working on the swimming pool. Inside, the dining room is being fitted.

Kelley strides from one activity to the other at a rapid pace with the aid of his cane. His quick glance will discover something not quite right. He breaks off whatever he is saying to the reporter to give correcting commands. Then he picks up the interrupted interview without missing a thought.

The blueprints are in his head, from the fractions of inches on door measurements to the various thicknesses of plaster on different walls.

The new hotel would have four bars and two dining rooms. One subterranean bar was to have an underwater view of the swimming pool through a huge picture window beneath the diving board. Another Kelley first.

"Cocktail sippers," stated the article, "can watch the swimmers frolicking in the water like fish at an aquarium."

With the completion of the new hotel, Roy moved his desk from the Edgewater lobby to the Reef Hotel lobby, repeating his dictum: "I don't want any upstairs office and secretary keeping me away from people."

The ten-story Reef was the first highrise on Waikiki Beach. "It was controversial because it rose above the tree line," said Richard. "But it was an instant success from the day it opened. The rooms had great views and the prices were dirt cheap compared to the other accommodations on the beach."

An annex of eighteen stories, the Reef Towers, was almost immediately started across from the new hotel on Kalia

Road. It would add 466 rooms to the growing Kelley inventory.

The most famous cigar box story, among many, involved the main restaurant at the Reef. The manager was a person who never impressed Roy as having a great deal of intelligence.

Before going on a long vacation, Roy sat down the manager.

Roy: "Here is a cigar box. It has $2,000 in cash in it. You pay for all of your supplies and your help out of this box. You put all of your receipts back into the box.

"If the box becomes empty, what do you do?"

"I don't know, Mr. Kelley."

"YOU CLOSE THE RESTAURANT, YOU DUMMY!"

When the family returned from vacation, there was only $200 in the cigar box. The manager was assigned the sole job of polishing a delicate part of a statue in the restaurant.

He was not so dumb that he didn't understand that it was time for him to seek employment elsewhere.

He did.

The Matson Viewpoint

Arthur Fiddy came to Hawaii in 1952 as the chief administrative officer for the Matson Hotels: the Royal Hawaiian, the Moana, the Moana cottages and, later, the Princess Kaiulani.

Matson Navigation used the hotels primarily as destination conveniences for their ship passengers.

Fiddy: "Our hotel rates were lower than they should have been because the important thing was to make the ships profitable and we needed desirable hotels at this end to do so. The ships cost a hell of a lot more than all the hotels put together.

"The rate at the Royal Hawaiian was $32 a day, double, and that included breakfast, lunch, and dinner with dancing in the Monarch Room.

"I had heard of Roy Kelley in San Francisco because

The Diamond Head beachfront home purchased from Dr. Fred Alsup in 1941 shortly before the attack on Pearl Harbor.

The Outrigger Canoe Club with the Royal Hawaiian Hotel in the background became the site of the Outrigger Waikiki in 1967. It was a major step forward in the emerging Kelley Hotel empire.

The complete Kelley
family, Roy and
Estelle with Richard,
Jean and Pat, leaving
for California.

The first Kelley Hotel in 1947. The four-story Islander Hotel with an added penthouse.

In 1951, the Kelleys opened the six-story 100-room Edgewater Hotel incorporating the first swimming pool and automatic elevators into an Hawaiian hotel. Note the added Kelley penthouse. The Edgewater replaced the Kelley-owned Willard Inn.

Estelle Kelley was the entire first reservation office
staff and the sales and marketing department.
Note the spindled holder hanging on the wall by her
right shoulder for holding future reservations.
When reservations measured three knuckles high,
she stopped taking them.

Tommy Perkins holds Maylyn Johnson at her christening. In the background are Lynn Ossipoff,
Roy Kelley, Estelle Kelley, Allen Johnson and Charlotte Johnson. Pat Kelley and Jean Kelley are
the two girls in the center of the photo, with Valerie Ossipoff and Sandra Ossipoff to the right.

Roy and Estelle were among the first frequent flyers. At the top of the stairs is Bob MacGregor, the first president of the newly established Outrigger Hotels.

Family portraits. Young Dr. Kelley with his bride, Jane Zieber Kelley, Roy, Estelle, Pat and Jean on the way to Europe in 1956. "Jane was newly pregnant," remembers Jean, "and threw up behind every monument in Europe."

Pat, Richard, and Jean stand behind their mother and father.

Roy and Estelle meet Chuck and Jean
Rolles returning home from Chuck
Feeney's wedding in Paris. Chuck
holds his son, Scott, while the proud
grandmother holds her six-week old
granddaughter, Kiki.

The Second and Third Generations and Spouses - 1988.
Front row: Linda V.G. Kelley, Kathryn Carey, Jenny Kelley, Bitsy Kelley Black, Mary Colleen Kelley, Linda Jane Springmeier, Estelle Marie Kelley, Michelle Norstrom, Pat Kelley, Kiki Tidwell, Susan Rolles, Jean Rolles. Back row: Richard Kelley, David Carey, Chuck Kelley, Scott Springmeier, Pete Petrequin, Bruce Tidwell, Scott Rolles. Not pictured: Christopher and Anne Marie Kelley.

Matson had agreed, around 1947, to turn over the lease on some property on Seaside Avenue to him. He wanted to expand the little cottage compound he had built just after the war.

"He was a budget builder because he had to be. He would forego some of the more expensive items in order to get the essential structure built and then add the niceties later.

"He'd trim wherever he could to get enough money to pay for the cost of two or more additional units. He was a hard working guy who deserved everything he got.

"Roy was a man who would watch his funds very carefully. He used to finish rooms on lower floors and put customers in them and take the money and put it into the new construction on the upper floors.

"When Roy Kelley finished the first building of the Edgewater Hotel, his rates were so low they didn't compete with ours.

"In 1953, we started building the Princess Kaiulani Hotel. I remember while we were building, Kelley decided to go with the second wing of the Edgewater. While he was showing me through it one day I said, 'The tile you are putting in the bathrooms looks familiar.' He laughed and said, 'They should, those are seconds from the Princess Kaiulani.'

"Always thinking. All of the time. A very capable man.

"Most people in the hotel industry are used to first class organizations. Everything on a high management level. They never went through the basic hands-on problems Kelley went through. He is a lot more capable than a lot of people give him credit for."

In 1947, when the little Islander Hotel opened, the visitor count was 25,000.

In 1951, the islands were being serviced by four-engine Stratocruiser aircraft from the West Coast.

In 1951, Kelley's Edgewater and Matson's Surfrider were added to Waikiki's hotel inventory.

By 1951, the visitor count reached 50,000.

In 1955, when the Reef Hotel opened, the Waikiki Biltmore, the Princess Kaiulani, and Kaiser's Hawaiian Village also joined the list of new hotels.

The visitor count in 1955 was 108,000.

CHAPTER FOUR

The Mushrooming Dynasty ...
The Skal Scandal ...
Allen Tours

The seven-year period between the opening of the Reef Hotel and the time when Roy Kelley leased the site of the old Outrigger Canoe Club next to the Royal Hawaiian Hotel was a time of frenetic development.

Roy Kelley: "We were really rolling then."

The rapid expansion was impressive.

After the first unit of the Reef Hotel came the Reef Hotel addition, bringing the total number of rooms in the complex to 885. Then came the Reef Towers and its cloned addition (466 rooms), followed by the Reef Lanais (110 rooms), The Waikiki Surf West (110 rooms), and the Coral Seas (109 rooms).

The old Islander Hotel on Kuhio Avenue was torn down and its name transferred to the 350-room Waikiki Surf Hotel.

The swift development by the Kelleys, the size of their properties and the way they operated changed the way the Hawaii visitor industry categorized itself.

Historically, accommodations in Hawaii had been divided into two classifications: 1. hotels with more than 100 rooms and 2. hotels with less than 100 rooms. With the advent of Roy and Estelle's pricing policy, it became common practice to refer to the "Kelley hotels" and "the others."

It became common practice for the local hotel industry to spin off of the low rates set by the Kelleys. It still is. As late as 1960, a person could find a cottage accommodation at the expanded Islander Hotel for $5 a night per person.

Sparks of controversy were not uncommon.

During a room shortage crunch, Roy Kelley opened 109 rooms in the first unit of the Reef Towers. Special rates were offered to guests, according to one newspaper account, "because the Tower did not have hot running water." Kelley said hot water would be available the next day.

"They can't do that," Howard M. Shima, the city building superintendent said. "The thing is incomplete."

The hotel was cited for violation of the city law for opening without an occupancy permit.

A hotel colleague laughed when reminded of the incident.

"Roy would be cited and pay a $150 fine and just go on about his business. It happened all the time. The city was so inept. What was a $150 fine?"

Another infamous controversy of the Fifties focused on the "Martini Club," a sobriquet given to a group of hotel leaders who met on occasion to discuss mutual problems. There was the *official* Hawaii Hotel Association made up of hotel executives, associates and suppliers, then there was the *unofficial* "Martini Club" of key hotel owners and managers who frequently met for breakfast. Of course, no one drank martinis at breakfast but it made good press headlines when the group was accused of fixing hotel rates.

The "Martini Club" included Roy Kelley, of course, and Henry Kaiser who had moved to Hawaii to occupy his "retirement" years with a twenty-acre hotel development he called The Hawaiian Village. Today, it is the Hilton Hawaiian Village.

Keeping the beaches clean, security, the general state of

business, beach boy discipline, perhaps even common union problems would be natural subjects for discussion. But not room rates.

No one competed with Kelley hotels on room rates.

The Great Topless Scandal

The Skal Club, an international trade organization made up of travel industry leaders, also met at regular intervals. Hotel owners, managers, sales and marketing people, airlines executives, tour operators and travel publishers belonged. The top cream of the tourist market ... with an all-male membership at that time.

One monthly meeting held in the Reef Hotel was to become world famous within the industry.

Bob MacGregor, president of Trade Wind Tours, tells his version of the evening.

"This had to be twenty years ago. That evening we had three topless waitresses. Twenty years ago that was *not* the thing to do.

"I called Roy in his Reef Tower penthouse. He wasn't a member of Skal because he was not a joiner. I said, 'Hey, Roy, come over here. We're having a little fun.'

"'No,' he declined, 'I'm in for the night.'

"But I pushed him. 'Come over for a little while, have a couple of drinks and meet some people.'

"He reluctantly said okay. He came over and his good eye popped out of his head because these were really good looking babes, you know, with little short bikinis and no tops.

"During the proceedings I picked up one of these girls and put her in Roy's lap. He didn't know what to do, you know. Anyway, when the cocktail hour was finished, Roy left, and while we were having dinner, one of my boys came up to me and said, 'Hey, we got problems.'

"'Why? What's wrong?'

"'Well, one of Roy's holier-than-thou maids has called the police and they have picked up the girls.'

"I tried to soothe him. 'Okay. Go down and pay the fifty bucks bail and forget it.'

"He said, 'It ain't that simple. *One of the girls is sixteen years old.*'

"'Holy cow!'

"So, the next day, the hotel gets cited by the Liquor Commission for indecent behavior in one of its bars. Roy gets called up to be his own witness and the head of the Liquor Commission says, 'Mister Kelley, you knew there were topless girls in your establishment. You saw them.'

"Roy objected: 'You know I am blind in one eye and I only have dim sight in the other. I didn't see anything.'

"But they fined him anyway and took his Reef liquor license away for about three days.

"The rest of us chipped in and presented him with a check for $1,000, which we figured it cost him, and he turned around and gave the money to charity."

Harry Meyer, owner/operator of a small hotel on Beachwalk near the Edgewater, was the person in charge of entertainment. He was also in charge of bailing the waitresses out of jail.

Meyer: "It was really no big thing. The girls had plumeria leis pasted around their chests and big leis strung around their necks. Even by the standards of those days it couldn't be considered indecent. Suggestive, maybe, but not indecent. What I remember most was that it was the foreign airline carrier executives who went down and personally protested to the police. Not the local guys, but the foreigners who showed some class.

"Now, a very coincidental thing happened. Some time prior to the Skal Club incident there had been a Stag Night at Oahu Country Club and one member brought along a new Polaroid camera. A novelty at the time. Otherwise, there wouldn't have been any camera allowed. Well, he took several pictures including some of the young ladies who were hired specially to serve as topless waitresses.

"On my way out of the stag, early in the morning, I saw a Polaroid picture lying on a table and, really, without thinking, I stuffed it into my pocket.

"After the Skal Club incident happened, because I was chairman of the entertainment committee, I was also cited on charges of contributing to the delinquency of a minor. The charge, which I thought would be dropped, wasn't dropped and I became concerned. Here I was, the father of five daughters being brought up on charges of contributing to the delinquency of a minor. Definitely not cool.

"So I called Neil Blaisdell, then the mayor, who was godfather of several of my children, and said I had to see him. I went to his office. And I told him about the problem. Then I showed him the Polaroid picture I had picked up at the Oahu Country Club Stag Night.

"The picture showed one of the delicately clad young ladies standing between His Honor and Robert Dodge, the public prosecutor.

"'The minor involved in the Skal Club incident,' I said, 'is the one standing next to you.'

"That's the last I heard about the problem."

Another person present at the Skal shenanigans was Bob Allen.

Bob Allen, also a Los Angeles High School alumnus, had come to Hawaii almost directly from a Philippine war prison camp.

He went to work for Earl Thacker's transportation company, the Gray Line Company, becoming, after a short time, its general manager.

"When I first arrived in the Islands, Roy still had his office in the old Islander Hotel on Seaside. He was then in the process of building the Edgewater. I asked him, 'Roy, what are you going to do with this hotel of yours? You are going to go up against the big boys? The Royal? The Moana?'

"'Oh,' he said, 'they won't be competition to me. I will build rooms that the average person can afford. My hotel will take care of people who travel on an economy budget. I think that is Hawaii's future market.'

"He was 'way ahead of his time.

"Let me tell you a personal anecdote. He had opened the Edgewater and I had booked a relative, Malcolm Williams, and his wife into the hotel.

"I picked the couple up at the airport and took them to the hotel. Malcolm had several bags and the hotel was quite busy. Roy was there walking around the front desk and there were no bellboys around so Roy went over and picked up my cousin's bags and took them to the elevator and carried them upstairs himself.

"Now, he didn't introduce himself and my cousin didn't know what to do because he looked more important than a bellboy. Malcolm was about to hand over a tip when I tapped him on the arm and shook my head.

"When Roy went out, I said 'Malcolm, that's the owner.'

"When I later recounted the story to Roy I wanted to know what he would have done if my cousin had offered him a tip?

"Roy never blinked before assuring me, 'I would have taken it.'

"When he was in that horrible accident, everybody went down to the hospital. Lyle Guslander, Howard Donnelly, Jack Fishbeck, Ernie Albrecht, Bryan Renwick. We were a closely knit industry fraternity. Well, he was propped up in a cast with parts suspended on pulleys. He looked like a space-man. He still had his sense of humor. He never lost that. Or his sense of business. Even in bed he was talking about his next project.

"Roy Kelley was always doing things for people behind the scenes. He never wanted his good deeds known. I think he liked having a tough reputation." Bob Allen paused, then added, "And he *was* tough. Tougher than hell.

"Kelley, Guslander, Child, they were all of the same mold in relation to their employees. They used the lash on them. The thing about Roy was that he'd know when to lay on the lash and when to lay off. He'd work somebody over pretty good and then, later on, he'd do something nice for them. That's just the way he was.

"I remember one fellow who was a terrific hotel man. He was particularly good on the front desk and excellent at administrative work. But he had a drinking problem. He'd work for four or five months and then go completely off the wagon. Roy would fire him as a matter of course. But he'd come back to work for Roy because, when he was sober, he was the world's champion.

"Well, one day this fellow did something Roy didn't like and Roy started working him over in front of guests ... the employees ... everybody.

"The fellow very calmly went on taking keys from the desk and putting them into slots, registering guests, doing this and that. All the while Roy is bawling him out. Loud and clear. The tirade went on for about five minutes.

"Finally the fellow looked over at Roy and asked, 'Roy, is it time for coffee?'

"And Roy said, 'Okay.' And off they went together for coffee."

Another Kelley story of the same nature has Roy Kelley dressing down a young bellboy in the lobby, again vociferously clear. Then Roy Kelley stepped back, smiled and said, "I suppose you think I am the meanest old bastard in the world."

Timidly, the bellboy replied, "Oh, Mr. Kelley, I don't think you are *that* old."

The smile of reminiscing disappears from Roy Kelley's face when he recalls another incident involving Shizu Kotano, a long time, loyal office employee who was dispatched to the bank one morning to draw out $30,000.

A robber stuck a gun into his back as he left the bank. Kotano turned around to give the robber a karate chop and the robber shot him. The bullet went through his spleen and the over-zealous employee died on his way to the hospital.

"It was only $30,000," Roy shakes his head at the pittance.

"What Roy doesn't tell you," Allen fills in, "is that he went to the widow and told her she would never have to worry again. He would take care of her. And he did. Roy never forgot his key employees or his friends.

"Loyalty was a Kelley trademark."

In 1945, a used car salesman without funds and in need of a room approached Roy. He was a war veteran with a debilitating illness that would put him in and out of Tripler Hospital for forty-four years. And for forty-four years, until his death in 1989, the Kelleys provided Jack Shelton with shelter.

Charity was another Kelley trademark.

A New Plateau

A key development in Hawaii tourism was signaled in 1952 with the arrival of the first large organized tour group. Chartered by the *Oregon Journal,* one hundred and fifty visitors came to Waikiki and were lodged in the new Edgewater Hotel.

The tour arrival also marked a change in the character of Hawaii visitors and hastened the fulfillment of the evolution from class to mass, or low budget, tourism predicted by Roy Kelley.

Bob MacGregor was a key player in the Hawaii leisure market changes, and also in the Kelley saga.

"Back in 1950 when I was just starting out with Trade Wind Tours, Kelley was building the Edgewater Hotel. I got the idea that I'd like to operate a travel desk there. Roy agreed, and I had the desk in the lobby for something like $150 a month.

"Shortly after the hotel opened I handled the first big tour from the *Oregon Journal* that came by air. I booked them into the Edgewater Hotel for three weeks. Roy kept watching how I operated and decided that I was a fairly honest Scot, dedicated to my work. He especially liked the way I paid my rent on time.

"When the Reef opened, he gave me that travel desk as well and then the Reef Tower opened and I got that travel desk too."

Meanwhile, Bob Allen was getting restless at Gray Line and broke with Earl Thacker to start Allen Tours.

Bob Allen: "With the coming of the first tour groups it seemed obvious to me that now was the time for Hawaii to have sightseeing buses. I had been up on the Mainland and had seen what the big boys were doing in L.A. and New York and other tourist centers, and I had my heart set on a glass-topped air-conditioned bus.

"So Bob MacGregor, Roy Kelley, Leong Hop Loui and I became stockholders in Allen Tours. Leong Hop Loui, a former sports writer for the Honolulu Advertiser, had joined Mac-Gregor to build International Travel, a separate company, into the largest travel agency in the state.

"Well, at first the banks didn't believe that tour buses were here to stay as far as Hawaii was concerned and we couldn't get financing. Eventually, Bob and I went down to Bishop Bank — before it became First Hawaiian — where a guy by the name of Bob Hyde agreed to finance the bus after I showed him all the literature from the Mainland and the history of where, what, and how much sightseeing buses were doing. Bob and I scraped up enough for a down payment and put our personal signatures on the line.

"The first bus cost $38,000. It was a thirty-three passenger bus with a deluxe interior. We had a little mini-bar in it and, going around the island, hostesses aboard served coffee and cakes.

"I had a great publicity idea for the launch of the first bus. I went to Jack Fishbeck at the Royal Hawaiian Hotel and I said, 'Jack, I'd like to have a little party and, as part of the party, I'd like to put a bus in your Surf Bar.'

"His mouth dropped about six inches, then he said, 'Allen, you have to be out of your mind.'

"But you had to know that Jack was a swinger. 'Jack,' I said, 'you know this publicity is going to be good for the Royal too.'

"He wanted to know how I was going to get a thirty-three passenger bus in the Surf Bar without damaging the property.

"I knew where there was leftover landing matting used in military airports during the war and I explained that if I brought the bus down the access road beside the Moana Hotel to the beach and then used the matting on the sand, I could roll the bus down the beach and into the Royal Hawaiian Hotel. And that's what we did. Took it right into the Surf Bar.

"That was the beginning of Allen Tours which, in essence, was a bus company. We called the bus the Pali Cruiser 1, and then brought in Pali Cruiser 2, 3, and 4. We were committed to bus transportation as tour groups began to come in.

"One of the first tour operators to bring in chartered groups was Transocean Airlines. Ed Hogan, who now owns Pleasant Hawaiian Holidays, was a tour conductor then. I always used to go down to meet him on incoming planes although they usually arrived around two or three in the morning.

"Transocean eventually went bankrupt. They owed Roy Kelley a lot of money. But I knew they were shaky and I told them the first time I didn't get paid their passengers could catch the public bus. They always paid me pretty much on the nose.

"In this period, just before starting Allen Tours, Roy caught me after we left a Rotary luncheon. As we were walking down the street he said, 'Bob, how would you like to be president of my hotel company?'

"That was flattering, so for about a year and a half I was president of his hotel company." Allen's laughter at the memory reverberated around the room.

"It didn't take long to realize that 'being president of Roy Kelley's hotel company' was, well, like being president of that wall over there. Roy Kelley had his own idea about everything and was not particularly receptive to other points of view.

"I got along fine with Roy but I never went to the mat with him. I knew enough not to cross him and not to make any suggestions about how to operate the hotels.

"He was always going to build me an office but, of course, he never did. Bob MacGregor would keep asking me, 'Well, is your office finished yet?' It was never started. We used to laugh like hell over that.

"Eventually, I went to Roy and said, 'All I am doing is signing a check now or then or signing documents I don't understand. You certainly don't need me.' So we shook hands and then I just went full time into Allen Tours.

"Then Gray Line made me an offer I couldn't refuse. Roy took me up to his penthouse suite and we sat there for about two hours while he tried to talk me into staying with the ship. But I went back to Gray Line. It had to be one of the great bad decisions of all time."

Allen Tours became Trade Wind Transportation Company and was sold much later to Greyhound Bus Company for several million dollars.

Publicity, Good and Bad

About this time, a major controversy was created when Roy Kelley, appearing before the Honolulu City Council, testified against an ordinance that would require an increase in off-street parking areas for new hotels and apartments.

Kelley charged in his testimony that stringent regulations were making it harder and harder to build in Waikiki, from an economic standpoint.

"Tourists do not use cars," Kelley was quoted in a newspaper article reporting the hearing.

"You can prove it by looking at the existing hotel parking lots at night when they are nearly empty. You are going to turn the place into an asphalt jungle for beach bums."

He went on to contend that additional parking was not needed and to increase the number of parking places would be to decrease areas which could be landscaped to preserve Waikiki's beauty.

In another newspaper story Kelley is quoted as jokingly suggesting that Waikiki be walled off at both ends and a "hula curtain" be erected to keep out local people. No one would be admitted unless he carried a "genuine tourist pass."

Fireworks!

"I had to field all the irate telephone calls," remembers Mildred Courtney, then the chief telephone operator. "It was terrible. The things that people said!"

The remark inspired a famous Harry Lyons' cartoon in the Honolulu Advertiser labeled "Kelleyland."

The cartoon illustrated a barricaded Waikiki with flag-pole banners proclaiming "Republic of Waikiki" and "Aloha to Our 51st State." An entrance gate was designated "Checkpoint Kelley." A fence sign advised that "Relatives and Friends of the Tourists May Visit on Christmas Day."

A blowup of the cartoon is on the wall of one of Roy Kelley's 'retirement' offices.

A serious continuing proposition championed by Roy was the conversion of Kalakaua Avenue into a pedestrian mall, diverting auto traffic to the Ala Wai Boulevard as Waikiki's new main traffic artery.

The City Council killed the plan after long debates and several public hearings in City Hall.

There were bright spots in the Kelley publicity history too.

In the Sixties, Roy Kelley created an Episcopal Chapel in the Reef Towers which was described as "a friendly, warm retreat where weary souls may rest awhile from turmoil of the street."

For the first four years the vicar was the Reverend Stanley Adams. On the chapel's fourth anniversary he praised the landlord: "The fulfillment of this much needed ministry was made possible through the generosity of Roy Kelley, owner of the Reef Hotel, who donated the space in which the chapel is located. Mr. Kelley has been wonderful. He has given us everything we want."

In the chapel's early days, according to the newspaper story devoted to its anniversary, Kelley sometimes would ask

ND
REPUBLIC OF WAIKIKI
LOHA TO
UR 51ST STATE...
TOURISTLAND!
HILTON TOURIST VILLAGE
BATTLE STATIONS! HERE COMES THE ROYAL WAIPAHU AIR FORCE!
ROYAL MALIHINI HOTEL
TOURISTS ONLY!
BUT I'M ROY KELLEY
STOP! DIS MEAN YOU, BRUDDA
RELATIVES AND FRIENDS OF THE TOURISTS MAY VISIT ON CHRISTMAS DAY
KEEP DIGGING!
KEEP OFF THE ~~GRASS~~ MINES
Harry Lyons

Party time in late 1940's: the Honolulu Architects Beaux-Arts Ball. Estelle Kelley is at far left. The sultan, center, is Roy Kelley with Burleigh Bauer on his right. Ed Bauer, with striped turban, kneels at far right while attorney Jinky Crozier kneels at center left. Violet Gaspar, wife of physician Louis Gaspar, stands above Ed Bauer.

The famous Harry Lyons cartoon depicting "Kelleyland."

Rev. Adams, "What was the 'take' this week, Reverend?"

"I'd tell him and he'd say, 'Heck, I got a parking lot doing better than that.'"

Besides scheduled Episcopalian services, the chapel was used by many other denominations. Hundreds of war veterans will remember the chapel as the place where they were married in Hawaii during their R&R leaves from Korea and Vietnam.

The Second Generation Comes Aboard

The late Fifties and early Sixties were landmark years for members of the Kelley family as well. Richard Kelley was graduated from Stanford with straight A's. He married and went on to earn a medical degree from Harvard Medical School. The new Dr. Kelley finished part of his pathology residency on the Mainland and returned to Hawaii in 1962 to finish his specialty training.

Jeannie Kelley came home one summer vacation from Cornell Hotel School with a sweetheart, Chuck Rolles, to work in the family hotel and returned a year later as Mrs. Rolles.

As Chuck remembers this history: "because Jeannie had not been home for Christmas for about four years, we came out to Hawaii to spend a month at Christmas in 1957, still newly-weds."

As Jeannie recalls it: "At the end of the month, I said, 'Okay, let's go.' But Chuck didn't want to leave. He said that Hawaii was going to be a state and there were many opportunities here in the hotel field. He said, 'I think we should stay.'

"I cautioned him, 'I don't want you to stay because my father is a very difficult person and I don't want to be the in-between. I don't want you blaming me when you find him intolerable.'

"He said, 'No. That won't happen.'

"I said, 'You will be upset with no change of climate. You'll be miserable when the leaves aren't falling in November and the snow isn't there in December.'

"We stayed."

Chuck: "Roy Kelley had convinced me that, because I had my Cornell Hotel School degree and education, I should give the hotel business a try for a year or so. He said I would learn a lot, whether I liked it or not.

"I worked for Roy Kelley at different jobs for about a year.

"I started in purchasing: liquor, soaps, sheets, arranging laundry contracts, things like that.

"The toughest job I had was working as a food purchaser for the main dining room. I was coming in at six in the morning and leaving at eight at night.

"All the salesmen were trying to meet me because I was the son-in-law, you know? It was a little strange for me because I had been the Big-Man-on-Campus at Cornell and here I was Roy Kelley's Son-in-Law in Hawaii. It was kind of a heavy thing.

"Well, I was telling the salesmen to just tell me what they were selling and go away because I was still trying to figure it all out. One day this salesman came in by the name of Joe Dacey. He was trying to be friendly and he asked where I was from. I said it was a little town in New York he had never heard of, and he asked what town, and I said Binghamton.

"He said, 'I'm from Binghamton.' He had played basketball ten years earlier at the same high school where I had played. We became good friends and he really helped me when it came time to open the first Chuck's Steak House.

"Once, I went with Roy Kelley to the Bank of Hawaii and we met with Ed Schneider who was the president and his assistant, Frank Manaut, who later became president. The four of us were in this room and Roy was talking about a loan — like five million — and Schneider said the interest rate would be six percent.

"Roy Kelley said, 'Well, I thought it would be five percent.' "Schneider came back and said, 'Let's split the difference, five and three quarters.'

"And Roy says, 'Okay.'

"That was my introduction to the big time."

Chuck took a sip of coffee and went on.

"When Roy built the addition to the Edgewater Hotel, he took the plans of the original building which had included a restaurant and simply flipped them over. As a result, he had all the plumbing and wiring for a second restaurant but in the opposite corner of the new building.

"Roy wanted a restaurant in there so he talked to Buzz Schneider who had Buzz's Steak and Lobster House right up the street. Buzz didn't like the idea for a number of reasons and turned it down.

"So a couple of days later I went to Roy and said, 'I'd like to take that space and do a restaurant.'

"He said, 'You don't want to do that.'

"I said, 'Yeah, I do.'

"Finally, he agreed to let me have a try. Well, Lyman Blank had a house up on Diamond Head Circle and I went up there one night for a party. He had split sisal that looks like small bamboo lining his swimming pool patio which he didn't like and was going to throw it out. I thought the sisal would make neat wall panelling for the restaurant and asked if I could have it. He said, 'sure.'

"Roy had a carpenter by the name of Nobu at the restaurant site when the sisal came in. He said, 'Now, Nobu, I want you to put this wood up so it can be taken down easily because Chuck will probably last here only about three weeks.' He says this while I am standing there. That's the way he was, you know.

"On the opening night, Lyman Blank came in with a couple of friends and that was our total dinner count. The second night we did eight dinners. But from the third night on, it was very successful."

Chuck's Steak House introduced a new feature to Honolulu diners: the salad bar. Build your own salad from a wide assortment of fresh ingredients.

Also, the waiters and waitresses were all fresh and young and wore Bermuda shorts, crisp white shirts and pristine tennis shoes. It was a new look for Honolulu.

Rolles continues: "Roy financed the restaurant but it

didn't cost him more than, maybe, twenty thousand because everything was in. He got the money back by charging a higher rent, like ten instead of six percent of gross.

"Originally, I had a business license but used his liquor license. Later, I got my own liquor license.

"Roy took a keen interest in my operation. He would even come down on Sunday morning and watch me cut steaks and estimate how many ounces in each steak.

"Then Jeannie and I went to Aspen, Colorado and opened a restaurant, and then to Los Angeles, and then La Jolla.

"When I came back to Hawaii my relationship was different with Roy Kelley. He said that I probably would never work for him again but he was pleased with what I was doing.

"At the high point, we had about fifty restaurants across the country. I originally thought that if you opened a restaurant with halfway decent food you could go on forever, but I was wrong. The restaurant business is very fickle. Lots of restaurants just die a natural death.

"My original idea of a salad bar and young, bright waiters and waitresses dressed casually has been copied by everyone.

"Now, I have about twenty-five restaurants, many of them Mexican which is more in line with what is happening today.

"Roy does like the stock market. He has a great attitude towards stocks. He told me his theory about buying stock. He'll buy a thousand shares of a stock at $20 and count on eventually having an average cost of $15 because, when he buys, he expects the stock to go to $10 and then he'll buy another thousand shares.

"It is all a game.

"He is notorious for not caring about material things. Or dress codes. He left for a cruise with Estelle one time and he had on one brown sock and one blue sock.

"I'm really happy and pleased with the relationship that I have with Roy and Estelle. It is very special to me.

"My marriage to Jeannie didn't work out for a number

of reasons but they have been very understanding. Roy Kelley has always told me that he considers me to be part of the family."

Pat also returned to Hawaii with her first husband, Dick Norstrom, who worked as a do-everything night manager, sometimes day manager at the Islander Hotel while attending the University of Hawaii.

"Working in the hotels," Pat remembers, "was a family tradition. We've done everything. All of us have. Clean rooms, scrub toilets, work the front desk, hand out keys.

"I worked in the reservations office for a long time with Mama. Filing ... lots of filing. Typing.

"When I divorced Dick, Mama got mad at me so Father said, 'You go to work over there.'

"Well, 'over there' was the Trade Wind's desk in the original Reef Hotel. It was managed by Margaret Eubanks who greeted my assignment with, 'You can sit here and not do a damn thing or you can work, I don't care. You are Kelley's daughter and I just have to put up with you.'

"I was so damned mad I said, 'Margaret, I'm going to have your job some day' and, by God, if I didn't. Eventually, I became manager of that same travel desk. She kicked me right where I needed it.

"Finally I got fed up because Daddy was always lecturing us about being 'service oriented.'

"'Be happy with the clients.

"'Say yes to the clients.

"'Figure out what the clients want, and then do it for them.

"'Don't give them twenty reasons for saying no.

"'Don't make them unhappy.'

"I went to Daddy with a proposition to start my own business. 'I think I can do better.' He sat there and laughed at me. Just laughed uproariously.

"'All right. You can have a desk. You pay a hundred dollars a month rent and you can set up your desk over there.'

"I asked, 'Where will I get a desk?'

"He said, 'Get one of the card tables out of the bridge room.'

"So I sat up a card table at the front of the lobby, went to Bob MacGregor — Bob was very understanding — and I said, 'Bob, I'm starting my own business in competition with you. Can I borrow your ticket stock.' He said, 'Sure.' So I used his ticket stock for three months and used his ticket machine until I had enough money to buy my own. Every time I made a sale, I used to run over to Daddy's desk and use his telephone. At the end of three months I had my own ticket stock, my own telephone and had a new desk built.

"I had no trouble selling Trade Wind Transportation Company tickets because, by then, Daddy owned half of the company. I did a lot of Outer Island bookings, too, and I went to the Guslander organization to be accredited to sell their rooms. Well, there was this dragon lady running it."

Myrtle Lee?

"Myrtle Lee. She sent back a form for me to fill out asking how much money I had, and everything like that, and saying I had to put up a bond.

"So I took the papers to Daddy and said, 'What do I do with this?'

"He took the papers and wrote across them, 'I personally guarantee every ticket my daughter will write.'

"That's how Pat Kelley Tours got started. When I sold it out to the family organization, which renamed it Outrigger Tours & Travel, Inc., it was grossing $6 million a year."

The Dragon Lady

Myrtle Lee is a sharp, vivacious, exotic Asian beauty who lacks only the long cigarette holder to perfectly fill the role of the Dragon Lady in the stage version of "Terry and the Pirates."

She's a delightful dinner companion, a competitive tennis player and an energetic dancer who also just happens to be a no-nonsense, hard-nosed business operator. She worked, first, for Bob MacGregor as operations manager for Trade Wind

Tours for almost eight years and then went to work for Lyle Guslander in his fledgling hotel enterprise.

Guslander got his start in the Hawaii visitor industry with Matson Hotels as general manager of the Moana and, subsequently, the new Surfrider. (The Surfrider was integrated into the beautifully restored Moana Hotel in 1989.) He was a cigar chomping, brusque ex-marine and a close friend of Roy Kelley's. Roy still keeps a large framed picture of the two of them in his retirement office.

Having left the security of the Matson Hotels, Guslander built the first postwar hotel on Kauai, the Coco Palms. His innovative manager, and later his wife, was the diminutive and gentle Grace Buscher. She created any number of Hawaii's "instant" traditions, including the twilight torch-lighting ceremony heralded by the blowing of the conch shell to call guests as witnesses.

The all-island chain of hotels launched by Guslander eventually was sold to Amfac in 1969 for what was then a fortune, some $20 million in stock and cash.

Myrtle Lee: "I joined Gus in 1957 who, then, was operating out of the basement of the Reef Hotel. He had one small office for himself and a fairly decent sized office to house seven or eight people in reservations. Although he already had three hotels, he really didn't have two pennies to rub together. The offices were provided to him free of charge by Roy Kelley.

"He and Gus were basically two of a kind. They had the same idea: a manager shouldn't be locked in an office but should be in the middle of the lobby where he could see everything and talk to the guests.

"The Coco Palms Hotel on Kauai was the first, then the Maui Palms in Kahului, and then the Kona Palms opposite the Kona Inn on the Big Island.

"Gus and Roy Kelley used to have these jolly meetings.

"Finally, Gus got enough money to move into the building on Kalakaua Avenue that David Watamull owned.

"Funny thing. The day came for us to move and a truck

came to move our furniture. I remember Roy Kelley was standing there watching. When somebody put an old dilapidated chair on the truck, Roy pulled it down and said, 'No, that's mine!'

"So funny. He had given Gus years of free rent but wouldn't give up a chair that was worthless. Who were we to argue? I think it was a good five years he took care of Gus. No rent whatsoever.

"Another story. There was this character in Waikiki who used to go around with a red sash around his waist and dressed in a white suit. He came from a Portuguese family with a lot of money, but his mother was smart and put the son's money in a trust. He couldn't draw more than a few dollars a month out of the trust, and he would blow those right away. He was always destitute.

"Who took care of him? Put him in one of his special units? Roy Kelley. Not that the kid couldn't afford to pay but, somehow, he got underneath the Kelley armor touching the magic button to Roy's generosity.

"You know if you worked for Roy Kelley, you saw one person. If you socialized with him, he was another guy. When you did business with him, there was this third person.

"Then along comes some kid with money and no brains and you saw a fourth Roy Kelley. Roy Kelley, the marshmallow.

"When Gus built the Holiday Isle Hotel on Lewers he built a special bar in the hotel and called it Shipwreck Kelley's. Guess who after? He took Roy's picture with a hat and cane and hung it in the bar. When the hotel was sold, I got the picture to give to Roy. It hangs now in his office.

"By 1969 Gus was being courted by all the big names who wanted to buy his hotels. He had run out of the big bucks needed to continue expanding, so he sold to Amfac because he felt they would be more understanding of our Hawaiiana way of operation. Eventually, he had to move downtown to become a group chairman and they made me president of the local hotels in 1973.

"During the years, there remained a certain amount of

reciprocity between the Kelley and the Guslander operations because of the close relationship between Roy and Gus.

"If you were in the trade, you needed Kelley — although sometimes it wasn't easy.

"Even when I was a travel agent with MacGregor, Mainland travel agents would tell me that they didn't want to book with Kelley because, if their clients complained about the hotel they were in, Kelley would throw them out. Get out! He was running the highest occupancy in town. Nobody could top his rate — $8 or $10 — what did they expect?"

In 1984, after endowing the Travel Industry Management school at the University of Hawaii with a million dollar chair, Lyle Guslander died suddenly of a heart attack.

Eventually, Amfac sold the Guslander hotels and Myrtle now is president of Island Holidays Tours.

"We still sell a lot of the Kelley hotels. Since Richard has taken over, they've done a lot of renovations. Properties are looking much better.

"The prices are still terrific buys in today's market.

"To tell you the truth, as far as I'm concerned, any travel wholesaler who is not in the good graces of — or can't deal with — the Outrigger Hotels, isn't going to make it. You need that inventory."

CHAPTER FIVE

The Outrigger Canoe Club Caper ...
The Cinerama Deal ...
Enter Dr. Kelley

"Luck!" repeats Roy Kelley, slapping the table for emphasis.

"Luck," he insists, was the biggest factor in his success.

"Opportunities just kept being pushed in front of me and I snatched them up," he says again.

A reviewer of the Kelley chronicle from the first 38-room Islander Hotel in 1947 to the 3,000-room inventory in ten hotels in 1962 could discern quite easily a successful format combining several essential factors. Luck would not, necessarily, be among them.

The first factor was that Roy Kelley, being a brilliant architect, could build a hotel room at half the price of his competition. He saved on architects' fees. He saved on contractors' fees and profits. He bought directly from suppliers. He hired and supervised his own labor and tradesmen.

As Estelle points out, "When we were constructing a building, we knew that there were two costs we'd have to deal with, the cost of materials and the cost of labor — and nothing more."

If another hotel company built a room for $20,000,

and therefore had to charge $20 a night, which was the rule of thumb, Kelley could build the same room for $10,000 and charge $10 a night. There wasn't any competition in the modest room rate market that the Kelleys carved out for themselves.

Secondly, there was no fat, operationally, in the Kelley hotels. There were no vice presidents. There was no marketing department. No advertising department. No public relations department. The only advertising placed in the early days was a single full page advertisement in the Hotel & Travel Index. (The 1990 Outrigger Hotels Hawaii advertising budget was $2 million.)

The hotels offered no room service, no service directory, no guest amenities.

Thirdly, and perhaps most importantly, the hotels were run on the principle of front desk management. Roy Kelley operated from one front desk and visited every one of his hotels' front desks seven days a week, in addition to supervising the purchasing department, the personnel department, and the financial planning department. Each hotel "manager" operated from the front desk. There were no private executive offices.

However, a day in 1963 brought Roy Kelley his biggest opportunity — almost by chance. Luck? Perhaps.

The opportunity involved the expiring lease on the beachfront site of the Outrigger Canoe Club. It was a plum of a property wedged between the Royal Hawaiian and the Moana hotels and stretching from the best of Waikiki Beach to Kalakaua Avenue.

The Outrigger Canoe Club had agreed to move out of Waikiki proper to a new clubhouse site on the toe of Diamond Head, across from Kapiolani Park next to the new Elks Club.

The canoe club's Waikiki site was owned by the Queen Emma Foundation, but the master lease was held by the Waikiki Development Corporation, a Texas-based company owned by Clint Murchinson and Paul Trousdale. They wanted to sublease the land.

Sheraton Hotels, who had bought the Matson Hotels in 1959, so desperately wanted the property for a new hotel that the corporation president came out from Boston to head the Sheraton negotiation team personally.

Local officers of the Waikiki Development Corporation, Ron Deisseroth and H.W.B. (Hod) White, headed the seller's negotiating team.

After lengthy sessions, it seemed that a lease agreement had been reached. So confident was Richard Holtzman, then vice president and general manager of Sheraton Hawaii Hotels, that he publicly confided to his peers at an industry luncheon in the Monarch Room of the Royal Hawaiian Hotel that the deal was done, and that a formal announcement of the lease signing and plans for a new Sheraton Outrigger Hotel would be made the next day.

Loud applause.

There had been no secret about the ongoing negotiations. Nor did the negotiations prevent Roy Kelley from mentioning to Ron Deisseroth at a Rotary Club meeting that if any hitch developed in his Sheraton proceedings, he was certainly interested in the lease.

The next day when the Sheraton officials met with the Texas company's lease negotiators to review the final papers, the Sheraton team claimed there was a new clause in the agreement that called for an automatic annual rent increase of $20,000 after a ten-year period.

"Not so," replied the leaseholders. "It's been there all the time."

"Not so," said the Sheraton negotiators. "It is new, and we are not going to sign it."

"We are not taking it out," said the leaseholders.

"We are not going to sign," held out Sheraton. (It was rumored in the industry later that the Sheraton president prided himself on his keenness. Perhaps, whispered the trade with a certain amount of snickering, he had been "too keen.")

Ron Deisseroth left the room and called Roy Kelley.

"Are you still interested in the Outrigger property?" he asked.

"I certainly am. How much?"

"The lease is $250,000 a year with an automatic increase of $20,000 in ten years."

"I'll take it," said Roy Kelley.

Ron Deisseroth, according to the local wags, returned to the meeting and said, "Gentlemen, the property is no longer available."

Obtaining the Outrigger Canoe Club site triggered gigantic new impetus within the Kelley hotel organization. It was said that if the Outrigger deal had not happened, Dr. Richard Kelley would never have stepped into the management team and the Kelley hotels would have been sold eventually, and Roy and Estelle Kelley would have retired.

Instead, a fiefdom became an empire.

Bob MacGregor was to become an important player in the new direction taken by the Kelley hotels. He is a veteran of Hawaii's travel wars and a passionate polo player who seems to walk with pain from too many uncontrolled landings on polo fields. His bowed legs make him look like he was once six feet tall but was pushed down to five feet five, his legs splayed under the pressure. The glens of Scotland are written over his craggy face.

Bob MacGregor: "At the time of the acquisition of the Outrigger property, I had been working next to Roy Kelley one way or another for over ten years.

"He had gotten to trust me and because his son, Richard, was dedicated to doctoring, he turned to me as a possible successor. One day he called me in and said, 'I'm going to come over and pick you up and we are going to go see Ron Deisseroth and sign a lease on the Outrigger Canoe Club property.' So I went with him and signed the lease. Then Roy said to me, 'You are going to help furnish the hotel, operate the hotel, and finance the hotel.'

"Later he said, 'You are going to be president of the Outrigger. I remained president for about three years.

"There was no one like Roy Kelley to forecast the future. On the way back from signing the Outrigger lease, he said to me, 'You know, Bob, we will put the lobby upstairs and shops and restaurants on the street level. The downstairs floor will pay for the lease rent and the taxes.' He was talking about $250,000 a year.

"Today, those shops pay the land rent and the taxes three times over.

"One thing you have to put into perspective is that Roy wasn't well. After lunch he would have to go to bed for a couple of hours. He wasn't sure he was going to make it. That is the one reason I went in as his number one assistant.

"Finally, his own son diagnosed the problem. Roy had pernicious anemia. All he needed was B-12 shots. He gradually recovered.

"The time came for financing and Roy said, "You take twenty-five percent, InterIsland Resorts which owns half of your company, will take twenty-five percent, and my family will take fifty percent.

"'Okay, but how much do I need to make up my share?'

"He said, 'Only half a million.'

"I said, 'I don't have half a million.'

"'Well, meet with some of your people and get them to kick in.'

"So I stretched myself and got eighteen others in my organization into a voting trust, so they could only vote with me.

"We made trips to the Mainland and bought furniture, hired an interior decorator, hired a manager."

MacGregor sighed happily remembering the old days.

"Roy did some clever things. Like put the swimming pool right on the beach. He created a luau garden. Hired the best head beach boy to keep tight control; no rowdiness was to be tolerated.

"The restaurants were concessions but we owned the nightclub. We opened with Tommy Sands, who was married to Nancy Sinatra, as the lead act. Eventually, we found the Society of Seven Group, SOS, and it has been SRO (Standing Room Only) ever since.

"We opened the hotel in July, 1967. We had our $2 million of equity and a $3 million note from the Bank of Hawaii.

"Later that year we were so happy after the hotel opened to full occupancies we all took off for Africa ... on an aerial safari. The whole Kelley family, Roy and Estelle, Richard and his first wife, Jane, Chuck Rolles and Jeannie, and the architect, Ed Bauer and his wife, Daisey."

"In three and a half years, the note was paid off."

MacGregor shakes his head in satisfaction and goes on.

"Meantime, I had bodies to move and I wasn't getting service from Gray Line. That's when Roy and Bob Allen and I started our own transportation company. We brought in the first air-conditioned buses. Roy wasn't getting good taxi service, so we formed Trade Wind Taxi. We started a rental car service, Trade Wind U-Drive.

"A couple of years passed and Roy called and said, 'Now I have a lease through Ron Deisseroth from the Queen Emma Foundation for the corner of Kuhio and Kaiulani.' He gave me a chance to take a seventh interest. By this time I had the money so I could go it alone.

"This was just three years after getting the Outrigger lease. On that corner was a Shell station, a taxi stand and a parking lot. History repeated itself. On the way back from the signing, Roy said, 'Eventually, the parking at the hotel will pay for the lease rent.' He was right, as usual. So, we built the Outrigger East on that corner."

A local newspaper reported in 1969 that Roy Kelley was selling his hotels.

The Honolulu Advertiser on Friday morning, January 31, in big red letters, bannered: "KELLEY HOTEL 'EMPIRE' UP FOR SALE."

The evening Star Bulletin ran a smaller contradictory story under the headline: "NO 'FOR SALE' SIGN ON KELLEY'S HOTELS."

Both stories quoted Roy Kelley as saying that the hotels would be for sale if that right price came along but the buyer would have to have at least one million in cash.

A week later, the Advertiser ran another screaming red headline: "SALE OF KELLEY HOTELS DUE TODAY."

The story was partially true. Roy Kelley had sold three hotels to Cinerama: the Edgewater, the Reef and the Reef Towers. But he retained four properties: the Edgewater Lanais, the Islander, the Coral Seas, and the Outrigger Waikiki. And, he had another five hotels under construction.

Dr. Kelley Recalls Cinerama Days

"Both my father and I see our business running in cycles. In 1969, Hawaiian tourism was at a peak. Our hotels were running full and were at their most saleable position. At the time, we were under construction with the Outrigger East, Outrigger West, the Outrigger Surf, the Waikiki Surf, and the Coral Reef all at the same time. Commitments to the landowners and zoning deadlines made it imperative that we get the new properties finished.

"We didn't know where the financing was coming from. Not only that but we were adding almost two thousand new rooms and we didn't know where the guests were coming from.

"My father was sitting at his desk in the lobby of the Reef Hotel one day when this fellow by the name of Bill Forman walks in. Dad knew him slightly from previous visits. He was a Mainlander with a string of theaters, including the Cinerama Group, who saw the real estate possibilities in Hawaii and bought the Consolidated Amusement chain of theaters.

"Forman was interested in expanding his real estate holdings by buying hotels so the two of them went into the bar and worked out a sales agreement, virtually on the back of an envelope.

"I think the sales price was $44 million for the three hotel properties, with $2 million down. The rest of the deal was all paper.

"My father thought at the time he was getting a good price because business was so good. Forman was in the right position to pay the price because he had a huge loss carried forward from promoting Cinerama. He expected to take the cash flow generated by the hotels and apply it against his theater losses.

"Unfortunately, Hawaii tourism fell off sharply after cresting later that year. Interest rates were climbing. The result was that Cinerama couldn't make payments on the hotel loan and we began to take Cinerama stock in lieu of payments. We ended up owning a significant share of Cinerama.

"Eventually, we bought out the public stockholders, by which time we owned fifty percent of Cinerama and the Formans owned the other half.

"Over a period of time we agreed with the Formans that we didn't know a damn thing about running theaters and they came to feel, over the same period, that they didn't know a damn thing about the hotel business.

"So we agreed to a friendly settlement in which we re-acquired our hotels and they took back all of the Cinerama stock. The deal was quite amicable and everybody was extremely happy to resolve the situation. In 1984, after a fifteen-year involvement, we were all closed out and we have both done well since then, operating the investments that we understand."

Richard Kelley was never far away from the hotel business.

While at Punahou School, he worked on construction of the family's first hotel and, along with his sisters, did a stint at every job in a hotel after it was opened.

"I wasn't a great student at Punahou," Richard remembers. "As a matter of fact the head of the school, Jack Fox, looked at my record and said he thought there was a little college in the Midwest maybe I could get into. But I applied to Stanford and was admitted. That was 1951.

At Stanford, Richard became a straight 'A' student.

On summer vacations from Stanford and, later, Harvard Medical School, he would bring college pals home with him, often to work in the Kelley hotels. One special "pal" was a young lady, Jane Zieber.

"We got married as soon as I got out of Stanford but the summer tradition of visiting classmates continued through medical school. One classmate became a plastic surgeon in Tucson. Another one became an admiral.

"Dick Sanderson, a Harvard classmate, had a very successful summer. The transportation company that Bob MacGregor and Bob Allen set up with my father got into rental cars.

"So they said to Dick, 'Okay, kid, you have a bunch of U-Drive cars down there in the basement of the Reef Hotel. See what you can get for them.'

"Bob MacGregor had a lobby tour desk and he had hired a pretty young blond girl named Polly Reeder. She was the daughter of a United Airlines pilot. When Sanderson wasn't hustling U-Drive cars in the basement, he was courting Polly upstairs.

"Sanderson had a great summer because he not only made a fabulous return on the U-Drives but he also married Polly.

"He's now a cardiac surgeon and lives in Tucson.

"Our family always worked. It was expected of us. I have one clear memory coming home from medical school and working down in the basement of the Edgewater Hotel along with Jane, who was by then my wife. We were getting lamps out of cartons and putting on the shades. The basement elevator door opens and this guy looks out, takes in the scene of this couple working on the lamps and said, 'You must be Kelleys.' The elevator door shuts and he's gone.

"That's the way the summers went.

"While getting my medical degree from Harvard, I spent a year at Massachusetts General Hospital in Boston doing research in the pathology department. That counted for one year of residency. I then spent a year of internship at the University of California Hospital in San Francisco. Then one year at the San Francisco General Hospital which was part of the University of California System. That gave me a second year of residency.

"I completed my required four years of residency with two years as a resident pathologist at Queen's Medical Center.

"Eventually, four of us negotiated a separate contract with Queen's to provide their pathological services. This allowed me to work out a flexible schedule with my partners. But I stayed fully active for a long period of time, attending weekly pathological clinics and a weekly tumor clinic, for example.

"I didn't leave medicine until 1970.

"In the early Sixties I was never far away from the hotel business either. Often when I had a spare moment, I'd just go down to a hotel and sit by my father and watch what went on.

"I do that with my kids now. If they don't have anything to do, I say, 'Okay, you be my puppy dog for the day and follow me around.' It was — and is — a great way to learn.

"I also went to the hotel association's meetings. We all went to the American Society of Travel Agents meeting in Athens one year.

"Then one day my father called me at the hospital. He said, 'Richard, I have to talk to you. Meet me over at the Reef Tower.'

"Well, this was an unusual place to meet because my parents were living in a penthouse in the Reef Tower at the time, which meant this was in mother's territory. Normally, he tried to stay away from mother because she was always pushing him to slow down.

"When I got to the hotel he took me aside, out of the flow of the lobby traffic, and said in a conspiratorial whisper, 'Richard, we just got the Outrigger Canoe Club site. You have to help me tell your mother.' "

Richard leaned forward to emphasize his words.

"To understand his apprehension, you have to appreciate the full partnership role my mother played in the success of the Kelley hotels.

"I don't think that either one would have been so successful without the other one. They were a team.

"Sure, my father got most of the attention of the press because he was a dynamic, outspoken, hard driving guy.

"But just as important, in the background, and very much part of the operation, was my mother who was the mollifier, the calming influence. She was the one employees went to when they got 'fired.' She put them back on the job.

"She gave my father the secure base from which he operated. She was the person who kept the family together. The kids, the home, the Sunday waffle tradition were all part of her scene.

"In the quiet times everything was discussed, so where business ended and family life picked up was often quite blurred.

"You have to remember too, in those early days particularly, she just didn't handle reservations, she was responsible for sales and marketing as well. She *was* the Sales and Marketing Department. All of it. The all-important liaison with travel agents who filled the rooms was her territory.

"She was honored by ASTA in the Sixties as the Hotel Executive of the Year for her outstanding cooperation with travel agents. Which reminds me of a cute story.

"Once, while the family was on a trip to Europe, we checked into a downtown hotel in Rome. The rooms were not right. Things weren't working in the rooms. Things just were not up to my mother's standard, so with blood in her eyes, she went down to the general manager's office to read him the riot act.

"Well, as she entered his office she spotted an ASTA plaque on his office wall acknowledging the same honor she had received.

"Before she got into her tirade, she quietly said to the manager, 'I have one of those.' He looked at her unbelievingly, went to his desk, pulled out an ASTA book and flipped through the pages, stopped at a page and pointed at it with his finger, and then said with amazement, 'Why, you do!'

"Needless to say they ended chatting like old friends ... exchanging travel agent names they both respected, as well as experiences ... and, of course, everything in the hotel was quickly set right.

"So you can understand the importance of getting my mother's stamp of approval on the Outrigger deal.

"She was an essential partner.

"When we finally told her about signing for the Outrigger site, she pitched a fit. For days and days she was very unhappy about the situation because it meant an absolute major commitment. Eventually she said, 'I'd like to be part of this and help you along.'

"That cleared the way for us to go ahead.

"The Outrigger Waikiki project was a turning point in my life.

"I got involved in some of the activity of the Outrigger Waikiki as it was getting under way. I'd stop off early in the morning before going to the hospital. Take a long lunch hour and go back again, and then look in after work. I took a great interest in the development of the plans and some of the interior designs.

"As the shops were being laid out, one fellow said, 'We ought to have a liquor store in this spot' and Dad said, 'Richard, why don't you and MacGregor operate a liquor store here.' I said fine, and we teamed up with Dick Norstrom.

"Then he said to Chuck Rolles, "You put one of your Chuck's Steak Houses in this corner.' And Chuck said fine.

"And he said, 'Richard, since you're a doctor, I think we need a pharmacy in the hotel, too.' And I said fine.

"I was still working full time at Queen's Hospital but at the same time I was also taking night courses at the University of Hawaii. I took business law and finance, all the things I didn't get when I was in medical school. I had an inkling I was going to need this knowledge later on. I took all the insurance courses. I took the real estate course and passed the exams.

"By the time the Outrigger opened, I was part of the team.

"Our first manager was Howard Donnelly. He resigned after a year to start his own company."

Howard Donnelly had been manager of the Royal Hawaiian Hotel. While he was still manager of the Royal, Donnelly tells of Roy's needling; how guests would check into the Royal for a day and then check out to move into the less expensive Reef Hotel. Then, according to Roy, they'd spend their time writing friends and relatives from their Reef lanais, but on Royal stationery, saying what a great time they were having at the Royal Hawaiian Hotel.

Richard carries on.

"Not long after Donnelly's assistant, Mike Hickey, took over, my father, who was deeply involved in building the Outrigger East and then the Outrigger West, said he didn't like the way things were going under Mike. He said, 'I think you should go down there and just talk to Mike every day and find out what is happening. Keep a close eye on it.'

"I can remember that Mike Hickey had a big desk and I used to come and sit on the edge of the desk. We'd go over reports.

"Then one day he quit and we were without a manager. That turned out to be a transition time. After he left, I said to myself, 'I am only temporary here. I'm not going to sit in that big chair.'

"We hired a new manager in Puerto Rico but he had to clean up his job and then drive across the country. Several weeks went by and he didn't show up and I'm working off the side of the desk in the Outrigger office. We finally got word from him that he had accepted a better offer.

"That happened at a time when my work had gotten a little boring at the hospital. During the Sixties, the Kapiolani Maternity Hospital lost their pathologist. They had nobody to run their lab. Couldn't get a replacement so they called my boss at Queen's and said, 'Can you lend us a pathologist for awhile?' So I went over there.

"I took over an operating room where I think I was born and turned it into a new laboratory. I kept a fairly close track of the economics of the lab and once a month I would go down to the head of the hospital, Dick Davi, and go over our profit and loss statement and show him how much money his lab made. Then I would hit him up for the next piece of equipment or the next staff person I needed. That was fun and exciting.

"It was about the time when the Outrigger was having its management problem that I went back to Queen's Medical Center. I remember walking in and I had this big stack of slides to look at. Tedious work. My mind was really on what was going on down at the hotel so I thought to myself, maybe I am in the wrong place.

"That's when I moved into the big chair.

"And twenty years later, here I am.

"To go back to my father, I think I was like a lot of his employees. I was very much afraid of him because he was volatile and demanding when you got into his space. Yet, there was a great deal of affection there and I wasn't so afraid of him that I wouldn't go down in my spare time and sit with him.

"It was very important, however, that I first establish my own identity. I did that.

"Nevertheless, he is still looking over my shoulder."

The shift of activity and responsibility from Roy to Richard over the period of almost two decades was gradual but steady, matching the continued growth of the Outrigger Hotels.

Richard started as Secretary/Treasurer. Then, sometime in the Seventies, he became President. He forgets the year because titles were of no importance in the Kelley family operation.

It was not until 1989, in fact, that Richard Kelley assumed the title of chairman and chief executive officer.

"As I look back on it now," continued Richard, the hotel man, "the extraordinary feat that was accomplished was the smoothness of our transition.

"My father was a very strong authority, accustomed to being the sole leader, dictatorial, unopposed.

"But he knew things were going to have to change and the success of that transition is a great tribute to him.

"During this entire period, my father was doing what he had always done while my responsibilities were constantly growing, yet there was never any written organizational chart, or anything like that, that laid out what my father would do and what I would do. When two strong personalities work together, they tend to get quite territorial. I see it among my own people. But my father and I maintained a very informal type of operation. And it is really amazing that we never got in each other's way.

"When I came in and took over the hotels bearing the Outrigger name, which included the Outrigger Waikiki, the Outrigger East, Outrigger West and Outrigger Surf, there was no conflict as often happens between a father and son when the son wants to do it one way and the father has always done it another way. That's the heart of family conflicts.

"We both tried very hard to avoid the problem.

"Every once in a while my father would come by and say, 'It's up to you how you run this thing but if you ask my opinion — .' Or he'd say, 'I wonder if you considered this — *but it's up to you.*'

"Ours was a very unique kind of relationship. And it worked.

"One reason it worked was because I had gone off and earned my own badges, my own identity, in a totally different field. He respected that and accepted me as an equal. So we could meet on a common ground.

"I didn't try to get into the architectural business and he didn't try to get into the medical business. That is, with rare exceptions."

Richard, the doctor, chuckles at a small transgression.

"Every once in a while a person would come up to the front desk and ask for Dr. Kelley and my father would end up listening to the medical problem. Fortunately, it was mostly the unimportant take-two-aspirins-and-call-me-in-the-morning kind of problem.

"Essentially, the story of the Seventies and the Eighties was of two fairly strong personalities who found a common ground through mutual respect and mutual interest. Although I ended up doing some things differently, on my part I looked at a system that had worked and tried not to change it for change sake. I have been very, very cautious about changing basic systems that have done so well over the years.

"At the time I became fully involved, there were, basically, three hotel entities. The Outrigger hotels were my responsibility. The Lewers Street hotels — the Waikiki Village, Coral Seas, Waikiki Surf and Reef Lanais — stayed under my father's wing, and the third division, the Cinerama hotels, remained under Bill Forman's management although, by the late Seventies, we were full partners with Cinerama.

"When I first sat in the big chair at the Outrigger Waikiki the operations were already in place and running. But with the Outrigger East, West and the Surf, we had to develop management teams and get the rest of the systems up and going.

"A few years after that — I forget the exact date — my mother finally said that she wanted to get out of the day-to-day work and have time to relax. She cut down her activity in reservations until she just plain stopped, but my father kept on being very active and very interested.

"In 1982, the Prince Kuhio deal came up. Just as my father had told Dr. Fred Alsup that if he ever wanted to sell the Diamond Head house, and just as he told Ron Deisseroth that if he had trouble negotiating the Outrigger Canoe Club site, he had called a principal of the Prince Kuhio, Bill Pruyn, to express his thought that it would be a troublesome operation, and if Bill ever wanted to get rid of it, please call him.

"So the time came when Bill Pruyn called my father and the two of them got together. Father set the price of $40 million and I handled the details from then on.

"An important part of that deal was labor negotiations.

"Then, in 1984, the employees of the Waikiki Village voted to decertify themselves from Local 5 and, with my experience at Prince Kuhio, I handled the labor negotiations for them. This was the first time I entered my father's territory.

"You have to remember that the years from 1980 to 1984 were very tough recession years. Hotel occupancies in Hawaii were not there. The rates were not there. The profits were not there. That's when the Formans decided that the hotel business was not their cup of tea and we took the hotels back.

"When we took back the Reef Hotel and the others from Cinerama, I handled those negotiations jointly with my father.

"The move meant biting the bullet and a commitment to major renovations which would require a lot of work and tremendous capital. For example, some of the Reef Hotel guest rooms still had the same wallpaper that had been installed in 1955 when the hotel was built – twenty-nine years later.

"With the Cinerama deal in the works, I knew we were going to have to merge our three divisions into one. I was thinking this through on a business trip to Tokyo when I ran into a corporate organizational consultant I had known for some time. Between meetings, we talked details and, eventually, he came aboard to help us reshape the company structure.

"Throughout the process of pulling all the hotels into a single entity, I took on more and more responsibility for the basic decisions ... although my father and I tried to consult each other when we were doing our individual things."

Richard's concern for his father's role is unmistaken.

"Really, the acquisition of the Waikiki Hobron was his last hurrah."

He recounts the episode with great affection.

"Two Waikiki hotels built during the Eighties' recession, the Maile Court and the Waikiki Hobron, were in terrible financial straits — really in bankruptcy. Both were owned by financial institutions.

"My father took a liking to one, and I took a liking to the other. We made an agreement that he would work on acquiring the Hobron and I would work to get the Maile Court. That was about 1986, which gives you some idea of his sustained activity, although by this time, I was really running the operations. He would still come in and make strategic suggestions and, typical of our relationship, there was no problem.

"I said, 'Okay, you work on the Hobron and I'll work on the Maile Court. If you need any assistance, I'll be here.' So I negotiated a direct buy-out of the Maile Court.

"However, the Waikiki Hobron was so far into bankruptcy that it was scheduled to be sold at public auction. It was not going to be a negotiated deal.

"Well, my father always believed that cash was king. No funny pieces of paper, like a check. So, during the six weeks leading up to the auction date, he had our central cashier pull out every hundred dollar bill received and replace it with a traveler's check ... or something else.

"Then came the day when we went down to the auction. I looked at my father — and gasped. He had bulges in his coat, in his shirt, in his pants. When he sat down or stood up, great wads of hundred dollar bills protruded out of every pocket. He probably was carrying $10,000 in $100 bills.

"His intention was to go to this auction with visible proof to show them that he was serious and that he had the cash to put on the barrel head to close the deal. I backed him up with the appropriate cashier's checks.

"Well, the bidding started. There were several interested parties at the auction ready to bid. The opening bid, by the financial institution that held the paper on the property, was for $20 million.

"My father immediately jumped the bid by $4 million to $24 million.

"Well, there was a buzz around the room and the gentlemen from the finance company excused themselves. They returned to the room in about three minutes and said they were not going to bid again. There were no other bids and the hotel became the Outrigger Hobron."

What a fitting exit to a bold and brilliant career.

Although Richard is now the chief executive officer, he meets with his parents two to three times a week over lunch and often drops by their Lewers Street gathering spot.

Jeannie and Pat also frequently attend their parent's luncheon table to share the latest progress.

There is much action to discuss. For example, the "garage sale" of six hotels in 1989 poured between $100 and $200 million into the Outrigger coffers. Of that, $125 million was earmarked for renovations over a five year period — $30 million each into the Reef and the Outrigger Waikiki alone.

There are busy times ahead for the family-held enterprise.

CHAPTER SIX

*The Stories of Four Veterans
in the Trenches ...
At the Front Desk*

"**U**nflagging**" would be the first virtue one would ascribe to the perfect Kelley Man. Or Kelley Woman. And, of course, ability.**

But to weather the storm of long-term Kelley employment took equal portions of dedication, the willingness to work long hours and unswerving loyalty.

In the long run, the Perfect Kelley Man or Woman received the utmost loyalty in return.

As always, as in the case of having served under the toughest military commander or commercial chief executive officer, the Perfect Kelley Man or Kelley Woman remembers his or her feared leader with unlimited affection and respect.

Winning always inspires loyalty.

When Kelley veterans recall days past, it is like talking to war veterans savoring their victories and reliving incidents that have survived as hilarious stories. There are a plethora of them.

Veteran Number One

Tom Burke is vice president of operations with offices in the Outrigger Hobron. Tall, his brown hair untouched by gray, Tom is the perfect hotel host. He is affable, his handshake is firm, his countenance pleasant. He looks you steadily and warmly in the eye from behind his spectacles. He is a professional greeter, capable of making every guest feel important and comfortable. In the best Kelley tradition.

He is in charge of three different groups of properties and responsible for the day-to-day operations of fourteen hotels.

"I walked into the Reef Hotel in 1966 looking for a job. I had been with army intelligence. Counterintelligence doing counterespionage work. I had gone directly into the military from college. Well, I couldn't find a job. There wasn't much need for counterespionage specialists in Hawaii.

"My folks were living up in Aiea in a home built from plans drawn up by Roy Kelley as a wedding present to the people who used to own the Marine Surf Hotel. My folks bought the house.

"So I walked in, introduced myself and said, 'Mr. Kelley, I'm looking for a job.'

"The interview lasted about two minutes, ending abruptly when he said, 'Fine. You're hired.'

"'When do I report?'

"'Tomorrow morning.'

"My first job was as a desk clerk. I worked from seven a.m. to three p.m. But then I would stay until about eleven because I was slow in my typing and, also, I wanted to learn the business.

"Three months later Roy Kelley walked up to me and said, "Young man, I want you to report to Tony Delpiano at the Reef Hotel tomorrow morning. You are now an assistant manager.'

"I said, "'Gee, thanks, Mr. Kelley.'

"He said, 'By the way, what's your name?' This, in itself, was quite a compliment because there was such a turnover of staff that he didn't think it was worth his time to memorize your name until you had worked for him at least six months."

Tom leans back in his desk chair and puts his hands behind his head, remembering his Kelley world as it was.

"I think I started at $300 a month but every six months he gave me a raise of $50 until I reached $500.

"The day Cinerama took over the Reef Hotel in 1969, Mr. Kelley came to me and said, 'Look, I'm going to need someone to run the Coral Seas, the Reef Lanais and the Edgewater Lanais hotels. Would you be interested in the job? I can't pay you anymore than you are making here as an assistant manager.'

"I told him yes, I would be interested.

"'Fine. Start tomorrow morning.' So I went to the Coral Seas the next morning at seven and Mr. Kelley was already there. He said, 'Okay, these are now your hotels.'

"'Great,' I said. 'How many people have I got working for me?'

"He replied, 'You're it. As far as the front desks are concerned, *you're it.*'

"'You mean, there is no one else at the other two hotel desks?'

"'You're it. It's up to you to find employees.'

"So, for a time, I had three hotels in the same neighborhood but, still, in three different locations and I was the *entire* front office. There were front desk phones at the Edgewater Lanais and the Reef Lanais and when somebody came to check in, I'd race over, register them, and run back again. I did that from six o'clock in the morning until the next morning at one o'clock. It was a madhouse."

Tom shakes his head in disbelief at the memory.

"Our house physician was Dr. Trager. He was on the board of directors of the Waikiki Shores, a hotel adjacent to the Reef. He came and offered me $1,200 a month to become manager of the Waikiki Shores. Well, I went to Father Kelley and told him about the offer and that it was pretty hard for me to turn down.

"He said, 'Look, we are going to be building three hotels, the Outrigger East, the Outrigger West and the Outrigger Surf. I'm going to pull Tony Delpiano away from Cinerama and he's going to open the Outrigger East and you can be the assistant manager and I will pay you $1,000 a month. Now, that is not going to be for a couple of years. I'd love you to stay but, if you go, I will keep that job open for you.'

"So I said that was fair enough but I had to think about it overnight. The next morning I came back and told him he'd given me my start when I didn't have a job and I would stay with him.

"Well, he was true to his word. The day the Outrigger East opened up, I was sent over to help. That was the day Roy Kelley fired me."

He FIRED you?

"He fired me!"

Tom's laugh reflected on a signal moment of his career.

"I had shown up at seven that morning and I was briefing the maids on what we had to do to clean up the new rooms and get them ready. The rooms had just been completed but there was still a lot of extra house cleaning details they had to look out for — scraping tiles, cleaning up leftover building dust ... things like that. Well, Roy Kelley shows up and he looks at the maids standing there and he looks at me and he growls, 'What the hell are you girls doing standing here? This is no way to clean rooms.'

"I tried to explain. 'Mr. Kelley, I guess this is my fault because I was briefing the girls on the extra things they need to be looking for in the rooms.'

"He snapped back, 'What time did you get here?'

"I said, 'Seven.'

"He said, 'It was light at six-thirty and I expected you to be here at six-thirty. You're fired.'

"So I went home. Stunned. I called Tony Delpiano, the manager, when he came in around seven-thirty and I said, 'Tony, I guess I have had the shortest career of any assistant manager you've ever had. Mr. Kelley just fired me.

"Tony said, 'Pay no attention. Come back to work.'

"I asked, 'Tony, are you sure?'

"He said, 'Yes. Just come back to work.'

"So I went back to work and not a thing was said for approximately a year and a half. The day I became manager of the Outrigger West Hotel, Roy Kelley came by and he said, 'Now you can show up at seven-thirty, Mr. Burke.'

"I think it's one of those delicious characteristics of Roy Kelley. Absolutely wonderful."

Tom changes the subject.

"Has anyone told you about the Roy Kelley traffic sheet? He designed the darn thing and every day he would come by the front desk, sit down with every hotel manager and review the 'traffic' in detail.

"The sheet had all the room numbers on it and when the room is ready you put an 'R' after that room. Out of order, you put three zeros. If the room is not ready, you put an 'NR.' After the maid cleans it up, you erase the 'N.' When you sell the room, you put a cross through the room number, write in the guest's name and the room rate.

"The room rate was a very flexible thing. One thing the managers had was flexibility in maneuvering the room rate. Roy Kelley's credo was 'some money is better than no money.' If a guest said he couldn't afford to pay a quoted room rate of $40 a day, Mr. Kelley would pop up and ask, 'How much can you afford?' And the guy would say, 'Gee, I can afford $20 a day.' Kelley would then say, 'Sign here.'

"At the end of the day the manager would add up the total tape on a little adding machine from the traffic sheets. The manager put together two piles. One pile for cash. One pile for credit cards. The two piles had to equal the total on the tape. It was pretty much a shoe-box operation. But the traffic sheet was the bible.

"At the end of the year, Mr. Kelley would look through his books and, if he thought you were doing a good job for him and your property was making money, the Christmas bonus he'd hand out personally was rather staggering. Like, at the Outrigger West, I started off making $1,000 a month. I can't remember what I received the first year but the second year he came in and gave me a check for $10,000 on which he had already paid the taxes. The third year it was $15,000.

"His philosophy was to give the money to you then and not down the line so you could manage your own affairs, buy a house or whatever. I was able in those days to buy a house for $27,000 which is worth around $300,000 today.

"He loves to play the stock market. He would come by and tell some of us, 'Such and such a stock is selling for $12. I think it is going to $30. Get some and sell out at $24.' We played that game with him."

Burke's smile reflected the financial gains that resulted from Roy's shared stock secrets.

"There is an unappreciated soft side to Roy Kelley. Like the time my wife left me. I was devastated.

"Roy Kelley came to me and said, 'Go after her and see if you can get her back. Take as much time as you need. As much time off from your job as you need. You will stay on full salary and your job will be here when you get back. If you need airplane tickets, we will buy you airplane tickets.' Well, I never got her back but I learned that I didn't have an employer, I had a great friend."

On the wall of Tom's office is a framed montage of various pictures of the Kelley family. Four generations. On top of the montage is a singular picture of Roy Kelley. It is a touching display because it is not based on sycophancy but on loyal devotion.

He continued on as he recalled another bit of Kelley lore.

"Let me tell you a typical Kelley 'manager' story. When we were opening the Outrigger East, Mr. Kelley was told that the union rate for hanging drapes was fifty cents a running foot.

"He said, 'I'm not going to pay that.' And he turned to me and said, 'You're going to do it. Let me show you how to hang drapes.' We went up to a room and he showed me how the tracks had been cut and how you wrap the drape around the edge of the track and raise the last pin so that end drape blossoms against the wall, making a nice tight seal to keep light out.

"He said, 'I think you can do this.'

"'Sure I can, Mr. Kelley,' I said.

"So I started hanging drapes and then, in the middle of the process, the union people showed up and said drape hanging is a union function and you can't do this.

"Mr. Kelley was very agreeable, basically saying 'Right. That's fine. Fine.' But when they had gone he turned to me with words to the effect: 'You Dummy, why didn't you hide from them? Now go back up but keep moving around the building so they don't catch you.'

"And that's what I did. I'd do three rooms on the fifth floor. Jump to the tenth floor. I kept moving around the building and draped the entire Outrigger East. Then, when the Outrigger Surf was about to open, I draped that entire hotel.

"Then Art Rutledge came around and Mr. Kelley said, 'Okay, Art, we will use your people.'

"But the bottom line was that Roy Kelley got two hotels draped with non-union Burke labor."

Manager Number Two

Tony Delpiano is officially retired from the Outrigger Hotels. His career with Roy Kelley started in 1957 and included work at the Edgewater, the Reef, the Outrigger Waikiki, the Outrigger East — which he opened — and the Prince Kuhio.

Tony is larger than life. Not physically. Emotionally. He talks with his hands, explodes his sentences, loving every laughing minute of voluble Kelley stories. His luxurious once-black hair is almost totally gray now but his eyes sparkle like those of a small boy.

"He's got this wonderful Italian mouth," one of his colleagues described him, affectionately. "Tony couldn't add two and two, but he made everybody happy."

Tony: "I was born in Rhode Island but was working in

Florida in the Fifties. The hotels there were still seasonal.

"Well, I married a girl who was born in Hawaii and we had two kids and I needed work all year long.

"A fellow with the Hawaii Visitors Bureau named Walt Wood stayed at our hotel and I asked him about the hotel situation in Hawaii. He said it was wonderful.

"So, with my family, I came to Hawaii in June, 1957, looking for a job. I was interviewed by Lyle Guslander who told me, 'The one guy you ought to see is Roy Kelley.'

"I made an appointment with Mr. Kelley because I wanted to do things right. At eight o'clock in the morning I was sitting by his desk when he came in.

"Well, we talked about two hours and he finally said, 'I think I can use you.'

"'Mr. Kelley, before you hire me you should know that your general manager at the Reef has already turned me down.'

"He said, 'I don't give a damn about the general manager. I'm the owner.'

"He made me assistant manager at the Edgewater Hotel across the street. I was there maybe three weeks and he liked what I did and how I worked. I worked nights, three in the afternoon until eleven p.m. I think he was paying me $300 a month. Anyway, after three weeks he moved me over to the Reef Hotel and he gave me a $50 raise.

"I figured I was doing good. I worked at the Reef three or four months and he came up to me and said, 'What day do you have off?'

"I said, 'Mr. Kelley, you haven't given me a day off yet.' So I got another raise. Christmas time came around and I got a $500 bonus. I had only worked for him for six months. The guy was," — and Tony throws his arms toward heaven for emphasis — "*tremendous.*"

"He was a tough guy to work for though, because he wouldn't take any nonsense and he had this reputation of telling people off and firing people. He could just look at some people and they would start shaking. I used to have employees call me up and ask me what kind of a mood he was in before they would go around to see him.

"At the Reef I was made assistant manager. I was working days when Mr. Kelley called me over and said, 'My night manager just quit so I'm going to put you on nights. It will only be for a short time and then I'll bring you back on days.'

"Nine ... years ... later" — Tony counts out the years with his fingers — "I finally went up to him and said, 'You know, Mr. Kelley, I got three kids and they don't know who their father is.'

"He said, 'I'll tell you what I'll do. I'll shift you to day shift for two days so you can see your family.' So I used to work four nights and two days. With Kelley, you worked six days a week.

"Then he finished the addition to the Reef and he put me back on days and it was beautiful, although when I was working nights, I tell you, it was fun.

"If guests had six bucks in their pocket and they needed a room, they got a room for six bucks. I'd fill a room for six dollars rather than let it run vacant. Not all of his night managers were diligent in filling rooms because it was just that much more work for them.

"I never looked at it that way. When Mr. Kelley came in every morning, I wanted a zero to show after 'rooms vacant' on the traffic sheet.

"As a matter of fact, after I had been on the day shift awhile, he told me, 'I'm losing five to six hundred dollars a day because you are not working nights.'

"When I moved back into days at the Reef, Mr. Kelley said, 'I'm going to build a desk for you in the lobby.'"

Tony laughs and shakes his head.

"I said, 'If anybody sits at the desk, it will be you.' That's the way it always was. He built a desk for me and he sat at it.

"When he built the Outrigger East, I went over there to open the hotel. Same thing. 'I'm going to build a desk for you.'

"And I repeated, 'And you are going to sit at it.' He did.

"Mr. Kelley — I always called him Mr. Kelley — and I worked side by side for about thirteen years, maybe three feet apart. Every conversation he had, I heard. Every conversation I had, he heard.

"I used to have to put pads of blank paper on his desk and #2 pencils. He always had a pad to draw on. If he wanted to explain something to you and, particularly if you didn't understand the problem, he would diagram it ... draw a picture.

"If it had to do with a location, the picture would start with a line down the middle of the pad and he would circle the top and say, 'Now these are the mountains.' Then a circle at the bottom. 'And this is the ocean. Got that?' School room stuff.

"Then he would say, 'You look at this long enough and you'll understand what I'm talking about.'

"He had a lot of nice friends. Lots of people came to him seeking advice.

"Most people don't know this side of Mr. Kelley: if you came up to him and said, 'I have three or four kids and we need a place to stay but I don't have any money,' Mr. Kelley would give you one of his cottages and say, 'Go sleep there. When you get a job you can pay me.'

"But if that same person checked in without telling him the situation first and then, after a week or so, announced, 'I don't have any money,' he'd get raging mad.

"He used to tell me when I first went to work for him, 'There are going to be a lot of people who will tell you they are friends of mine. Don't worry about them. Just do your job. Don't give them any special favors.'

"But, as general manager, if I wanted to do anything special for a guest, I knew I could always do it. I did. That's how you get guests to come back to you.

"One year, around early December, we had this guy in one of the Edgewater cottages. He had been there about two or three weeks and we learned he couldn't pay his bill. We were ready to throw him out. Then we find out he's playing Santa Claus in one of the stores downtown. So how do you throw out Santa Claus at Christmas? He stayed.

"When Cinerama moved in, Mr. Kelley told Cinerama they could borrow me for awhile. He had three new hotels he was working on. After I'd worked for Cinerama for a few weeks, the general manager came up to me and said, 'Let's you and I have lunch.' So we went and had a nice lunch and then he says, 'The reason we are getting together is that you and I are making the same money and the hotel can't afford that. You're going to have to take a $500 pay cut.'

"I said, 'You're out of your mind.'

"So after lunch I walked across the street and saw Mr. Kelley and told him what had happened. He tells me, 'Monday you go to work for the Outrigger Waikiki.' Hickey was still there. Then he quit. I filled in as general manager but I used to tell Mr. Kelley, 'You give me these fancy titles but I must be the highest paid room clerk in Hawaii.'

"If there is a Kelley motto, it would be '*Fill The Rooms.*'

"When Dick Edwards was general manager of the Edgewater, Mr. Kelley would come to work and ask Dick, 'How are we doing today.'

"Dick Edwards would say, 'We're sold out. We have no rooms.'

"The next morning Kelley would come down and the traffic sheet would show fourteen rooms vacant. 'How come fourteen vacant rooms? You said we were sold out.'

"'Some people just didn't show up,' Dick Edwards would explain.

"Finally, Mr. Kelley had enough of this and he consequently built up a little reputation for overbooking.

"I went through one Christmas I'll never forget. Mrs. Kelley, who was still handling reservations, cut off all reservations for Christmas. Well, it was about the twelfth of December, the lowest traffic spot in the year and we had about two hundred vacant rooms in the Reef Hotel — out of three hundred and fifty. Mr. Kelley asked me to get him one of the big picture postcards of the Reef Hotel. He writes this travel agent on the West Coast and tells him that the Reef is wide open. 'We got lots of room,' he writes him. 'Not to worry. Keep sending people.'"

Tony looks at the ceiling in horror.

"Come the twenty-third of December and we are a hundred rooms overbooked. Well, Harry Meyer's wife had a brother who had just completed a co-op apartment over on Ena Road. That was our salvation. We would send about a hundred people a day to the apartment house, bring them back to the Reef the next day, and then send the next hundred arrivals over. I tell you I never worked so hard in my life. Guests beat up on me all week long. Mr. Kelley never tried that again. I think Mrs. Kelley gave him a piece of her mind.

"When I was at the Reef, we were full almost every day. One hundred percent. We had a crazy system. Mr. Kelley didn't like me to ask people how long they were going to say. So we would get unexpected checkouts or, more often, guests would overstay their reservations.

"Still, Mr. Kelley would give us hell if we asked how long they were going to stay. 'Why do you ask when they are going to leave? They're just checking in. You want to get rid of them?'

"Meantime, Mrs. Kelley was going crazy in reservations. She would have a fit. She had no way of knowing what was happening. That's one thing that got straightened out when Dr. Kelley came on the scene and we went to computers.

"I lived on the desk in those early days. I had strict orders from Mr. Kelley, 'If I come up those stairs and you are not there, you're fired.' That was *always*. Even later, when Dr. Kelley took over, if I was upstairs showing a room, Dr. Kelley would come by and leave little love notes, 'Tony, I was here at 9:30. Where were you?'

"So I never walked the property that much. My concern was for those wonderful people waiting at the front desk.

That's what I cared about."

Tony leans forward confidentially. "Let me tell you one of my favorite stories. One time I went up to Mr. Kelley and I said, 'I just came back from Royal Hawaiian Hotel and they have a beautiful brass mail box in the lobby. Why don't you have a mail box in the lobby?'

"He was feeling good that day and my question amused him. He cocked his head to the side like he does and said, 'Because when you don't have a mailbox, people are going to come up and talk to you. They are going to ask you where the mailbox is. You are going to talk to them, find out where they are from, what room they are in, ask them about this and that, and you are going to get to know the guests much better than if we had a mail box. Don't worry. You take their mail and we'll have a mailbox under the front desk.'

"He was right, you know. I got to know lots of guests by their first names just because they wanted to mail a letter. I learned what room they wanted. What they liked to do. I even had this blind man from New Zealand who stayed at the Reef every year. He always wanted the same room. How did he know what room he was in? But he got the same room, religiously, every year.

"When you worked for Kelley, you worked long and you worked hard. The whole family works hard. I remember, once, Rutledge pulled a little strike on us at the Reef, a real walkout. Richard, Jeannie Rolles, Pat, all their kids, everybody was working down in the laundry or cleaning rooms. I never saw a family so close.

"In my dealings with Mr. Kelley, he had two books. He had the 'good' book and the 'bad' book. If you ever made the bad book, you could never make the good book. You were dead. I started off in the good book, I think, because I worked four months before I got a day off and I worked two years before I got a vacation.

"Why?"

Tony places his hand over his mouth in a gesture of not wanting to answer his own question. He removes the hand and says, as if to a confidant: "Because I was afraid to ask!

"Listen. One time when I was still working at the Reef, this guy came over and begged Mr. Kelley for a job. Begged and begged. For three weeks he begged for a job. Finally, Kelley gave him a job. He was building the Reef Lanais and Kelley says, 'Okay, I'm going to give you a job in security on the night shift.'

"Then he ticked off all the things he wanted him to do.

"The next day, Kelley sees the guy and asks, 'How did it go?'

"The guy says, 'It went beautifully.'

"Kelley asks, 'Did you do this and did you do that?'

"The guy says he has done everything and then — I can't believe my ears — he asks, 'By the way, Mr. Kelley, when is my day off?'

"Kelley bluntly answers, 'Today.'"

Tony is almost crying with laughter.

He layers on still another contribution to the Kelley legend.

"One day Mr. Kelley came up to me and asked, 'When was the last time you went home?'

"I said, 'Mr. Kelley, I have been with you on this island for thirteen years and I have never left. I have never been home.'

"He said, 'You got to go home. How much time do you want off?'

"I said, 'I come from Rhode Island. Maybe a month.'

"He said, 'Fine. You should go home.'

"He and Mrs. Kelley arranged it. Got all the maps for us. Everything. Thanks to them I got a real special deal on a Matson ship. Flowers and fruit from the Kelleys with a card saying, 'Have a good trip.'

"We were gone five weeks."

And still another.

"With my bonuses, I used to buy property. A Christmas bonus was enough for a down payment in those days. One day I went to see Mr. Kelley and I said, 'I want to borrow some money.'

"He said, 'Why do you want to borrow money?'

"I said, 'There's a piece of property I want to buy but I don't have enough money.'

"'Are you going to build a house on it right away?' he asked.

"'No, I don't have enough money to build a house on it right away.'

"'Well,' he says, 'why don't you wait until you have a enough money to build a house and then buy the property?'

"'Because,' I said, 'by the time I'm ready to build a house, the property will cost too much.'

"'How much do you need?'

"'About $7,500.'

"He walked away and came back later and hands me a check. 'Christmas came a little early this year,' he said. The check was for $7,500. Then, for Christmas, I got my regular bonus.

"It was no secret that Roy Kelley had money. Lots of money. You just never knew it by looking at him or talking with him.

"One time there were these guys from 3M checking in and we got talking about 3M. I said, 'Mr. Kelley, here are a couple of gentlemen who work for 3M.'

"So Mr. Kelley comes over and says, 'I had a chance to buy stock in 3M at one time.'

"One of the guys looks at him and says, 'You should have. You would have been a rich man today.' Afterwards, Mr. Kelley and I laughed and laughed. How little the 3M guys knew."

Delpiano's affection for his employer was undisguised.

"I was at the Outrigger Waikiki and Chuck Comeau

was at Cinerama. He wasn't happy and asked Mr. Kelley for a job and Kelley brought him over to the Outrigger Waikiki.

"Then the Outrigger East opened and I went over there where I had a desk," he paused momentarily before adding his usual post script, "but Mr. Kelley sat at it all the time. This was in 1972 when room rates were about $12 single and $18 double deluxe. Same as the Reef. In the winter, the rates would go up a couple of dollars.

"I was at the Outrigger East for eleven years. Then, in 1982, Dr. Kelley bought the Prince Kuhio when he was in charge of the whole Kelley operation.

"In July, I got a call from Dr. Kelley. He had just fired my night manager. He said in this low voice he has, 'Tony, when you are through work today, I want you to come to my office.'

"Well, I wondered if I was going to get fired. But he made me general manager of the Prince Kuhio and I stayed there until I retired in 1987. I still go in once a week. Keep my hand in.

"Thirty years with Roy Kelley. Friend said to me, 'You should have gotten a medal.'

"Oh, yeah. Those were the years. I got more than a medal. A whole lot of wonderful memories. Those were the years."

Then Tony says slowly, almost reverently, "He was like a father to me. A father."

Manager Number Three

Chuck Comeau today is general manager of the Outrigger Waikiki and vice president of Outrigger Hotels Hawaii.

"I had first met Roy Kelley when I came out to Hawaii on a two-week vacation after getting out of officer's training school. I stayed at the Reef and I remember Mr. Kelley sitting there at the desk most of the time. Several years later I came back to Hawaii, on assignment at Hickam Air Force Base, and I requested a stay at the Reef. Roy Kelley was still there and I commented on meeting him during my previous visit. He upgraded my room. Little did I realize that four years later I would be working for him.

"My first job in the hotel business, however, was not with Roy Kelley directly.

"I joined the Reef Hotel under Cinerama management as a management trainee. I worked in every department and saw lots of ways to run a hotel and lots of ways not to run a hotel.

"Everybody in the industry knew about Roy Kelley's method of operation. Practically everybody at the Reef, at that time, had been trained under the Kelley method.

"It didn't take me long to learn that Kelley's method of running a hotel was quite different from any hotel operation in the world.

"Roy Kelley had his desk right in the lobby, right?

"A Kelley manager was behind the front desk.

"The Kelley night manager was behind the front desk.

"Well, when Cinerama took over, they brought in a very seasoned boss who immediately set aside two lush suites at the Reef Towers for his office. And you never saw him. Certainly not Roy Kelley's style.

"Then the Reef Hotel's new general manager took over most of the guest rooms on the first floor and converted them into two offices — Ivory Towers really — remote from what was really going on. When I saw this kind of physical change, I began to appreciate Mr. Kelley's hands-on method of operation.

"At first it was exciting for me because I was just out of the Air Force. I was a captain, a general's aide. The hotel business was another world."

(Chuck Comeau still looks like a general's aide. His brown hair is immaculately neat, his figure is military trim, his shoulders are square. His demeanor is that of one on the alert, ready to jump at the general's request.)

"I was with Cinerama for about a year. When Mike Hickey left the Outrigger Waikiki and took many of his staff with him, Mr. Kelley had an opening there and offered me the position of night manager.

"I recall being interviewed by him in a little hole-in-the-wall office on Lewers Road. He had a card table for his desk with heaps and heaps of paper on it. But he knew exactly where everything was on that table.

"There are so many stories about Mr. Kelley. How he would fire this person or that person on a whim. I never came to find that to be true. I could certainly see he meant business and he could be very, very firm if it was required. No, he didn't scare me at all.

"He's never been tough or rough with me. Some people feared him so much that they would start trembling when he walked into the room. But in my case, it was never like that.

"Yes, people you talk to locally say that Roy Kelley has the reputation of being very lean and mean in his operation. Certainly he operated with a minimal staff.

"One of the reasons was because he stayed so close to the heart of the operations. He only saw with one eye but with that one eye he could catch errors or trouble spots so fast it was unbelievable. If he went through a night manager's report, he would invariably catch something.

"You know, when he hired me during that interview, he said, 'Comeau, you will always stay with me if you remember that you are never to be remote from the people you serve. You are going to be a manager, but that means a working manager. You are to lead and inspire your people and set the tone. I never want to see you away from the guests you are here to serve.'

"That has stuck with me all these years.

"When you have the responsibility for paper work, overseeing a large housekeeping department, maintenance, reservations, it can be draining. Especially doing that six days a week.

"But if you ring my office, and it rings three times, the call will be transferred automatically to the front desk because that is where I will be, particularly around the heavy guest check-in periods.

"I'm there. With over fifty-five percent of our business in return guests, they expect to see Chuck Comeau there. They expect to have the same room they had the last time. They expect a favorable rate.

"So I came aboard in 1971 about the same time that Dr. Kelley began to take over. Of course he was still practicing medicine and continued to do so for some time but he knew he had to step into the hotel business and start making important decisions that needed to be made.

"We now have a moving, dynamic company and we are really stepping into the 1990s under his leadership. Morale is up. It's wonderful.

"Now, we work six days one week and five days the next week. I took six days a week in stride for eighteen years but today, frankly, some of the younger managers were burning out on a six-day week.

"A few years ago the hotels were really looking tired. It's a whole different picture today. We have spent $100 million on renovations.

"My guest rooms are the best kept secret in Waikiki. My guest rooms are beautiful. Our front entrance doesn't do us justice but it is no secret that our occupancy runs tradition-ally ninety-five to ninety-six percent year round and we owe that to our legion of returning guests and friends they keep sending. And much of that business is direct."

Comeau is serious when he talks about his hotel.

He relaxes a little; a general's aide at rest.

"You know Roy and Estelle come here Monday, Tuesday and Wednesday for lunch. Thursdays, they go to the Prince Kuhio. Friday to the Tower. Saturday, downstairs with Al Batz at the Brass Rail.

"Before Mr. Kelley goes to lunch, he naturally looks at the room count. 'How many rooms do you have to sell, Comeau?'

"'None, Mr. Kelley.'

"'Good!' he says. That always makes him happy. For

years and years we have run full and I've always been able to tell Mr. Kelley that we are sold out tonight. Or, we are ten or eleven rooms overbooked. That pleases him even more.

"He pretty much leaves us alone at the Outrigger Waikiki because we are always full. But he likes to stand by the desk and hear the guests' comments, how happy and enjoyable their stay has been.

"Often, I will take the occasion to introduce the guests to Roy Kelley as owner and founder of the Outrigger Hotels. He likes that. Certainly at this point in his life, he enjoys being recognized. He's still sharp but he's really mellowed tremendously.

"I don't know what it is that is so unique about this man but he just has a way of gaining the loyalty of his managers and department heads that can't be matched. *If you can pass the test.*"

Chuck Comeau has been asked to move to the company's executive offices. He prefers to stay on the firing line, doing that which he knows best.

"I spend a lot of time answering personal letters for reservations and taking personal telephone calls for reservations.

"That's why I am at the front desk.

"These people want to see Chuck. They want that upgraded room and they want that special rate."

"Dr. Kelley comes by two to three times a week or so. He's a brilliant man, absolutely brilliant. Very businesslike. He's not as keen about 'the people side' of the business as his father was. But he's brought the company along.

"We now have profit sharing. We have a pension plan and we have a retirement plan. Dr. Kelley is good for all of us."

He cocks his head admiringly.

"But Roy Kelley will always be a model for me. A grasp of details, decisive, fast moving. He sure would have made a hell of a general."

Manager Number Four

Had she appeared on television's early show, "What's My Line," you might have guessed her a schoolmarm or a governess. She sits quietly, her back straight in the disciplined fashion of a gentler era.

Your "What's My Line" guess would have been wrong.

Mildred Courtney's demure manner, her sedately coiffed brown hair and a gentle countenance do not fit the portrait of a high-ranked hotel professional, but Mildred Courtney manages not one but four of the Outrigger Hotels: the Waikiki Surf, the Waikiki East, the Waikiki West, and the Outrigger Malia.

Mildred Courtney is a soft-spoken dynamo.

How did such a sedate lady become Hotel Group manager in an industry not known for women managers? And especially for an owner whose male chauvinistic reputation seemed to have been fairly earned?

She launched her thirty-five-year career in the Kelley organization as a telephone operator in 1955.

"I was born in Honolulu but raised on the Big Island. While going to high school, I worked part-time for the Hawaiian Telephone Company.

"My maiden name was Quintal. A French name but my father was part Portuguese, like most of the dairy farmers in Hawaii. He owned the Quintal Dairy which later became the site of the Waialae Drive-in Theater.

"Bill Kline was connected with the Edgewater Hotel when the Reef Hotel was under construction. He heard I was a good worker and asked me if I would be interested in going to work at the new hotel as a telephone operator.

"I said no, I was perfectly happy being a housewife. He asked me a second time. No, I said."

Life in Hawaii in 1955 was still relatively simple. There weren't the number of working wives there are today and the fledgling visitor industry did not require the huge numbers of employees it does today.

"Well, the third time Bill called I thought, 'They must

really need me.'

"So I begged my husband to let me take the job. When he said okay, I started at the bottom — literally. The Reef switchboard was in the basement of the hotel.

"It has been a very interesting experience, getting out of the basement.

"I was told that it was Mr. Kelley's policy to interview every new employee but he was too involved with the new hotel to interview me.

"I could tell just looking around me that he really liked *haoles*."

In postwar Hawaii, when the Caucasian (haole) ruled politically and economically, the Portuguese, although technically 'Caucasian,' were considered a race apart because they had been imported as a labor force.

"I didn't think I'd last two seconds once I had an encounter with him.

"For six months, my only contact with Roy Kelley was through the switchboard.

"When he was around, all employees were terrified.

"Whenever he talked to anyone, he referred to his employees as 'animals.' I just wasn't an animal and meant to prove it to him.

"Mr. Kelley thought the first thing he had to do every morning was to wake up everyone on the switchboard. He would pick up his phone, press the plunger down and then drop the phone and leave it off the hook. Then he'd go to the next phone and do the same thing, and so on until all the lights on the switchboard were lit.

"I knew he would eventually come back to the first one and I would be waiting for him. I was the brave one. And I would say, 'Good morning, Mr. Kelley.'

"I used to think, 'Gee, this is a really different human being. What makes this man tick?' I didn't have to put up with him if I didn't want to but I was determined to find out why people were so afraid of him. Why he was such a demanding man, a bully really.

"Six months after I started working I had my first encounter with him. He always thought I was this haole on the switchboard.

"He wanted to know who I was and was my husband in the service? I didn't tell him what my husband did. I was the employee and he didn't have to know what my husband did. I wasn't afraid of him.

"Subsequently, in the process of finding out who this Roy Kelley was, I found out — besides finding a hard man — I found a person with a very warm heart. But it took patience.

"I worked hard at my job. I wanted to show him that all 'locals' weren't dummies. Or animals.

"Roy Kelley was the sort of man who did everything on his own. Rather than relying on other people, he preferred to do a job himself."

Mildred remembers a favorite work story.

"He wasn't very articulate. When we asked him for a number, he would just mumble. None of the other operators ever wanted to take his calls because they couldn't understand what he was saying. I was the one who would always have to answer him.

"He would want to know how long I had been on the job. People never lasted very long around there. I would say, 'I have been here for two weeks, Mr. Kelley.' I always thought that was just enough seniority to get by. Then he would blurt out the number.

"Well, I would get the first three digits — there were only five digits in those days — but I would always miss the last two numbers. Then he would explode, 'Get me someone who understands English!'

"Since the other operators were afraid to talk to him, I would change my voice and say, 'Yes, Mr. Kelley, may I help you, please?'

"Well, on the second try all I had to do was listen for the last two digits. He never knew he was dealing with me all the time. This went on for months.

"Mr. Kline had a lot of confidence in me. It was he who

pushed me up. He was very positive and believed that I could learn quickly, which I did. He eventually put me in charge of the telephone exchange."

Becoming the head telephone operator was the first step out of the basement. Her abilities and hard work brought about increased responsibilities and pushed Mildred to the top.

Her second step upward involved Boat Days.

Boat Days were highlights of the week in Honolulu before commercial airlines linked Hawaii to the Mainland U.S.A. In addition to the Matson ships — *S.S. Lurline, S.S. Monterey,* and *S.S. Mariposa* — several other shipping lines also stopped in Honolulu on a regular basis.

On Boat Days, harbor tugs rocked in the surf beyond the reef waiting to deposit immigration officials, reporters, hotel and tour operators aboard the incoming liners to organize passengers for an orderly debarkation.

After the ships docked alongside the Aloha Tower in downtown Honolulu, local boys churned the water diving for coins. They'd surface, deposit the coins in their mouths, and dive for the next coin tossed overboard by the passengers.

The Royal Hawaiian Band would be at shipside playing traditional Hawaiian songs. Passengers hurled spirals of colorful confetti to the crowd on the dock. The air was festive and bubbling with excitement as relatives and friends arrived from Mainland journeys. Newcomers would be swept up into the magic of Hawaii through the smell of flowers, the sound of the band playing "The Hawaiian War Chant," and the sight of verdant green foliage everywhere, or an occasional rainbow.

At the foot of Aloha Tower handsome Hawaiian ladies lined the sidewalk stringing, displaying, and selling thousands of multicolored flower leis.

It was amid this environment that Mildred Courtney expanded her role in the Kelley organization.

Roy Kelley would not permit the free tourist publications in his hotels because they advertised competitive accommodations and restaurants.

"Mr. Kelley started his own in-house publication called The Waikiki Visitor," Mildred explains. "A bunch of us used to go out on the pilot's tug and meet the ships off Diamond Head to interview our incoming guests and take them leis. We called ourselves 'Tugboat Annies' and we had a ball.

"The interviews and pictures would go into The Waikiki Visitor because, as Mr. Kelley said, 'Guests always are happy to see their faces and names in print.'

"All I did was fill out where they were from and the reason for their trips. Just a little write-up.

"I got so good at it that I started to tie-in with the airlines. United Airlines at first. I used to give the airline a credit line in the story or picture and I would send stories and pictures to home town newspapers.

"One time I did a montage of all the employees as a greeting to our guests and Mr. Kelley came and told me I did a great job. That's the only time — I think — he told me I did a great job.

"By that time I was wearing many hats.

"I handled all the telephone cut-overs and consolidations. When they were opening up a new hotel, for example, we had to order new switchboards. I would do all the preliminary work, coordinating work with the engineers, making sure there was proper cable, etc.

"By this time I was working very closely with Mr. Kelley. He trusted me.

"From there I started taking care of all his appointments, particularly when he became involved in negotiating a big deal. Like when he sold the whole corner of Seaside and Kalakaua to Bill Mau. It was the biggest, best kept secret in Waikiki. I used to set up the appointments with Bill Mau's secretary.

"Ruth, however, always remained Mr. Kelley's official secretary. I became his 'Girl Friday.'

"I remember, he had all these little things for me to do on my way home. Stop by the map maker, stop here, stop there, do this and do that.

"For a while I was a trouble shooter. Whenever revenues were down at a certain hotel, he would test me, send me in to see what I could do.

"I worked at the Reef Lanais, Coral Seas and then I opened the Waikiki Surf which was very difficult. Getting the rooms ready and all, I never had had that kind of experience.

"After the hotel was opened, he said, 'Now you've got to get us $1,500 of business a day.'

"One of the first things I did was to go down to the airlines. By that time they had these little computer terminals for making reservations. I got to know the airline reservations people, chatted with them, told them about our new hotel and how hungry we were for business ... told them about our rates, that they were as low as $10 a day. I would come back with business in hand.

"That really shaped my sales skills. The only thing I disliked was dealing with taxi drivers — if they asked me about getting something under the table, I would pretend I didn't know what they were talking about — but I would go down and talk to them and they would bring me business.

"Then, during the Vietnam war, we had a lot of parents and girl friends and wives coming from the Mainland to greet soldiers coming in for rest and recuperation. I would go down to Fort DeRussy and come back with lots of business.

"I got Mr. Kelley his $1,500 worth of business a day."

Mildred Courtney sits quietly while recounting the past. Sometimes she breaks into a smile at a pleasant memory or waves a hand in an expression of dismay.

"The other managers didn't pay much attention to me but I was very close to Mr. Kelley. He depended more and more on me. Every time he wanted something, he would say, 'Get me Mildred.'

"He didn't think much of women but I stood up to him even though I knew when I went to work for him he was definitely a male chauvinist. But I never let that bother me.

He's my best friend now.

"Roy Kelley is conquerable.

"I remember back in 1952 when he was president of the Hawaii Hotel Association and he was in charge of the telephone committee. He used to drag me to the meetings with him, fancy luncheons, you know, and he insisted that I sit at the head table with him because I did all the dirty work. That was just his way of saying thank you.

"Once they had this big company bash for him at Diamond Head. When I arrived, I went to sit with the other managers. Dr. Kelley came over and said, 'My father wants you to sit at the head table.'

"So there I was at the head table with Mr. and Mrs. Kelley, all their children and my husband. The other relatives all wanted to know who I was and what I had going at the head table.

"Roy Kelley didn't have any hobbies except, perhaps, for the stock market.

"To this day, Mr. Kelley has the sharpest mind when it comes to the stock market. He got me into buying stock. I started with $5,000 and I know I have over $100,000 now. Once, he kept pushing me into a stock and I said, 'I don't have any money' and he said, 'I'll get it for you.' Well, I had a CD coming due so the money he put up for me, I gave right back to him. That was the first time — and the last time — I ever let him lend me money.

"He got me into long-term stocks. He would say, 'Buy this and if you don't want it anymore, I'll buy it from you.' And he meant it.

"One characteristic of Mr. Kelley's was, although he made tons of money in the stock market and he owned all of these hotels and lots of other real estate, he always acted like a regular person. He didn't want anybody to treat him any differently than anyone else. No ego at all. He was a very unusual man that way.

"Let me tell you story.

"My husband and I had a beach house on the other side

of the island. The property next door came up for sale. Well, we really wanted it but the bank turned down our application for a loan.

"I told Mr. Kelley how disappointed we were and he reached over and got a scrap of paper and wrote on it, 'This is Mildred Courtney, my closest employee. Give her whatever money she wants.' and he signed it 'Roy Kelley.'

"I took the note up to the Waikiki branch of the Bank of Hawaii where Larry Johnson was the branch manager. He's the president of the bank now.

"I got the money. There were no points. The interest rate was low and the legal department of the Bank of Hawaii handled all the paperwork without cost.

"It was a typical Roy Kelley gesture."

CHAPTER SEVEN

The Unions ...
Art Rutledge ...
The Hotels ...
Trade Wind Tours

"**W**hat was it like, Mr. Kelley, getting along with the Unions?" a friend asked.

"WAR!" bellowed Roy Kelley, the street fighter, beaming with pleasure.

"WAR!"

The union movement in the hotel and restaurant industry started in 1937 when the Hotel, Restaurant & Bar Catering Association of the Hawaiian Islands, Local No. 1 was formally organized.

The following year the independent local union received a charter from what was then the Hotel and Restaurant Employees' International Alliance & Bartenders' International League of America. Local 5, for years, was referred to as "the Bartenders" because the first efforts of the union were directed to the local bars where sailors would respect any union efforts, including strikes.

Also, in 1938, the Local acquired a new member transferred from San Francisco. A bartender named Art Rutledge, a cocky, short, pugnacious man who had been born in Poland as Avrom Rotleider, a subject of the Tsar of Russia.

Brought to America at the age of six, his parents separated, and his mother died when he was twelve. He and his brother went to an orphanage. He had taken care of himself since then, educated on the streets. An aggressive survivor.

Rutledge — without prior union experience — took over the union within a year of his arrival in the islands. He first served as financial secretary and then as business agent without pay.

Fertile ground awaited a union movement in Hawaii.

According to the pamphlet "A History of Local 5" published by the University of Hawaii in 1937, the majority of restaurant employees worked seven days a week, commonly more than ten hours a day. One woman in seven was paid less than 10¢ an hour. Men received more; they averaged 23¢ an hour. No tips. No vacations.

The hotel labor was not much better. Wages in hotels averaged $56 a month in housekeeping, $52.50 in the dining rooms (with meals included) and $77.50 in the kitchens (also with meals). Women in hotels earned from 18¢ to 41¢ an hour.

At the end of two years, Local 5 had obtained contracts with the Matson Hotels (The Royal Hawaiian and the Moana hotels) and the Alexander Young Hotel, and its membership had increased sixteenfold, growing from 40 to 640.

Later, Art Rutledge also became head of a second union, Hawaii Teamsters Union, Local 996, giving him control of all transit workers which included bus drivers and tour bus drivers, among others.

Rutledge's go-for-the-jugular aggressiveness won him a large army of enemies. But his keen business sense combined with his own complex, colorful personality also established for him another army of admirers.

"He knew when to hit, how hard to hit, and exactly when to settle," wrote one commentator.

The two unions shared headquarters in Unity House, a building erected in 1959 with funds from both unions. Unity House was organized as a nonprofit corporation with every dues-paying member as a stockholder.

As an investment, the corporation also built a hotel on its 36,000-square-foot fee-simple property which extended from Ena Road to Ala Moana Boulevard. The Waikiki Marina Hotel, built back-to-back with its headquarters, fronted on the Boulevard.

The Unity House office of Art Rutledge is large but plain. To one side of his spreading, paper cluttered desk is a coffee pot brewing on a hot plate. Alongside are paper cups.

Around the walls are paintings of eight men, three former union colleagues, four hotel executives and one well-known local investor. Six of the eight are dead; all of his union friends and three of the hotelmen.

"I call this the Room of the Holy Ghosts," says Art Rutledge, peering at the pictures through bottle-thick glasses.

Gone are Henry Kaiser who created the Hawaiian Village as a hobby in his so-called "retirement" years, Ed Hastings who headed Hilton's early regime, and popular Dick Holtzman who was responsible for Sheraton in Hawaii until he left to become president of the Rockefeller hotel company.

The fourth hotel man in the "Holy Ghosts" line-up, and the only one still alive, is Roy Kelley.

Art Rutledge: "I first ran across Roy Kelley over thirty years ago when he was building the Edgewater. I believe he had Doc Kelley working down there, digging or something, and I said to Roy Kelley, 'What's that haole kid doing there?'

"Kelley said, 'That's my son. He might as well work for it because he's going to get it all one day.'

"I forget the dates now. It must have been around 1951 or '52 when we won the right to hold a union election of the Edgewater employees. Now, I didn't know Kelley, except by reputation. Supposed to be a mean son-of-a-bitch. I was really fearful of this guy.

"Well, he hired the Hawaii Employers Council to represent his hotel against us. That didn't do him any good. We won the election.

"So after we won the election, he *had* to do business with us. Then he went off on a trip, saying he wasn't going to have any union guy telling him what to do.

"He had a fellow managing the hotel by the name of Dick Edwards, who he left in charge.

"So we sat down and tried to negotiate with Edwards. Jimmy Chock — you see his picture here on the wall — he organized the meeting. He was the union secretary then, and I was president. We didn't know too much about negotiating really and I could tell that Edwards didn't have much experience either. And I could see he was very nervous. You might say frightened.

"I told him, 'I think what we should do is forget about negotiating and wait until Roy Kelley gets back and he can decide for himself which way he wants to go broke.'

"So we waited until Roy came back and we sat down together. The first thing he says to me is, 'Tell me why you didn't want to talk to Edwards?'

"I said, 'Mr. Kelley, I didn't think he had any authority to do anything. He was all nervous because I think he is afraid of you. I figured that if he gave me anything, you would probably fire him, and, if he didn't give us anything and we called a strike, you would have fired him for that.'

"You've got to know Roy Kelley to appreciate this. He has this way of cocking his head, you know. Well, he cocked his head, thought about it a moment and said, 'You know, you're right.'"

Rutledge lifts his head and chuckles fondly at the memory.

"That was the beginning of our relationship. We got down to negotiating and eventually hammered out a workable contract. Before we signed the contract — a union person would appreciate this — we asked for what is known as a union shop. A union shop means that everybody working the place has to join the union after a month.

"Our proposed contract also had a check-off provision which means that monthly dues are automatically deducted off the individual's wages and forwarded to the union.

"I even weighed more then than I do now and Jimmy

Chock was about the same size and Roy Kelley says, 'Both of you fat asses can go out and collect your own dues. They got to pay your dues anyway.'

"When he said that, I realized he wasn't objecting to the closed union shop. So, in spite of the fact he didn't like having anything to do with us, Roy Kelley gave us the first closed union shop in the hotel business in Hawaii.

In the pamphlet, "A History of Local 5," author John Reinecke reported:

> *"Kelley, an architect, had gone into the tourist business, adding to the Edgewater, buying the old Islander Hotel and ten apartment buildings besides. He had no use at all for the union and he stalled as long as possible, claiming that the NLRB didn't have jurisdiction over hotels in a Territory. The NLRB ruled against him, and on August 1, 1951, Local 5 won bargaining rights, 42 to 12 out of only 66 eligible voters.*
>
> *Kelley was unpredictable. Having fought the union, he turned around and signed an agreement in record time, only six weeks after the election, and he gave us what we could not win from Matson until 1956, the union shop."*

Rutledge picks up their personal history: "We sort of hit it off after that. Came time to sign the contract and I changed it a little bit. He had a bartender and two waitresses and I put it in the contract that they didn't have to join the union but their replacements would.

"He said, 'Why did you do that? You mean, there are three people on my side?'

"Two weeks afterwards, he called me in and said, 'You know those people in the bar? I'm getting rid of them.'

"'Why?' I asked.

"'Because they didn't want to join the union,' he said

and laughed. Actually, I think, he had caught a bit of cash register jiggling going on.

"After he signed the agreement, I asked who in the personnel department would sign it. He said, 'No need. I signed it. Now you've got to catch me.'

"We used to meet here in my office about every two weeks because he never had an office, you know, just that desk in the lobby. Well, he would have a little list of our grievances and he would take pleasure of going over the list, 'Hah! You're wrong on that one,' he'd say.

"Then when it was all over, he would say, 'Hah! There are a couple you didn't catch me on.' And he would tell me about them, see.

"One day he came in my office with my son Tony following him. Tony was about twenty then.

"Kelley said, 'I brought your son in here and I want to tell you something. Tell him to leave me alone. Don't bother me. Just because I get along with you doesn't mean I like unions. Tell your son not to bother me about union stuff. I'll talk to you about it.'

Rutledge puts his hands on his desk and gives a deep sigh. As though on cue, the door to Rutledge's office opens abruptly and a burly man rolls in, looks unsmilingly around the room, and is introduced as Tony Rutledge. He exits without pleasantries.

Rutledge continues: "Then, early on, we gave Roy Kelley an honorary membership union card to Local 5.

"Roy Kelley didn't belong to the Elks Club or anything like that, you know. For years afterwards, when somebody would ask him if he belonged to this or that, he would pull out his union card which was in tatters by that time, and say, 'This is the only thing I belong to.'

Again, the deep infectious chuckle rolled out of Rutledge's throat.

"We built the Unity House at a time when Kaiser was building the Hawaiian Village and everybody was short of help. We built this six-story building when we had a permit for only three floors. So we were in violation.

"Kelley told me I should have known better. Anyway, we got the variance. Then, later, because we had enough property behind us to build a hotel, I asked Kelley, with his experience, to give us a hand building a hotel.

"So Kelley assigned a draftsman to do the drawings, see. His first designs were for apartments for union members. I told him that he might be a damn good hotelman but he didn't know anything about union guys because they would never pay the rent. So he just drew a line between two rooms, this little draftsman, and we ended up with twice as many rooms, 323. About 63 rooms had kitchenettes which was unusual. He got us off to a good start.

"We had all kinds of problems with the hotel and I would go to Roy Kelley for help. I remember telling him, 'Hell, I didn't know there were so many headaches in the hotel business. I thought I knew all about hotels but I don't know a damn thing.'

"Kelley said, 'I knew that all the time. Now you've learned something about being a capitalist instead of a unionist.'

"Years later, I think after Doc took over, I said to Roy, 'You know something I don't understand. Our rooms in the Waikiki Marina Hotel that you designed are all drab colored, not like the rooms Richard has in his hotels.'

"He thought that was funny as hell and he says, 'Didn't you know I was color blind?'"

Art Rutledge pushed at papers on his desk. His voice changed from that of the storyteller to a friend just fondly reminiscing.

"Kelley was supposed to be mean as hell. Maybe he'd bawl out a maid and then go up to the next floor and when he came down again, he'd smile at that maid like it was the first time he had seen her that day. He'd already forgotten about it.

"He'd help anybody who needed help, even people

who were in competition with him. There was a man who was not envious of anybody. Henry Kaiser was the same way. That's why I have their pictures up there."

Rutledge looks at each of the paintings momentarily and goes back to the storytelling voice.

"You know, Harry Weinberg used to have an apartment across the street and he would come in and use my office like he owned it. Put his feet up on the desk. Call his stockbroker. Harry Weinberg would never spend a dime if he could spend yours. Maybe the wealthiest man in Honolulu but the tightest man with a buck in the world.

"We were always arguing, Harry and me. You've heard the expression, there's only one thing two Jews can agree on. You know what that is? That's what the *third* Jew contributes to the Synagogue."

His laughter is robust.

"Well, I had these pictures finished of Kaiser and Hastings and Holtzman and Kelley. Harry came in here one day after I had put the pictures on the wall. Harry looked at the pictures and he had a hurt look, like a little boy that was hurt. His picture wasn't there.

"So I called his wife and asked her if she has a picture of Harry with a coat and tie on. If you know him, you know he only wears an aloha shirt.

"Well, she found a snapshot, it was probably on the day they got married because, for once, he was wearing a coat and tie.

"I had his portrait painted and hung it right over there next to Kelley's picture.

"Well, Harry comes charging in one morning while I am sitting here at the desk; he comes right over and starts using my telephone as usual and his eyes wander around the room — and he spots his picture.

"He hangs up the phone. Walks slowly over to the portrait. He looks at it up close ... real close. A minute goes by. Then he turns around and guess what he says."

What does he say?

"'How much did it cost?' That's Harry Weinberg for you."

Rutledge, still surveying the portraits, points to the one of Kelley.

"Getting back to Roy Kelley. If you notice, his teeth are a little crooked. When he came in and saw his picture, he did the same thing as Harry. Went over and squinted at it with his good eye for a long time. Finally, he turned around and smiled and allowed, 'You know, Arthur, I always wanted to have my teeth straightened and you did it for me.'

"People used to wonder about our relationship. We had fights —" Rutledge's body language shrugged them off as insignificant — "but they were only about dollars and cents.

"Respect was what really mattered. For example, when Jimmy Chock died, Kelley helped organize a little parade to St. Augustine's. He was there for the funeral from the beginning to the end.

"Once, right here in this room, a hotel committee came in to talk about a new contract. There was Roy Kelley, Len Gorrell from the Sheraton properties and somebody else on the committee. We were trying to negotiate a uniform industry agreement.

"Well, the union was proposing an eight cents hike for waiters, waitresses and the room maids.

"Kelley said, 'See, you don't know anything about hotel people. Those waiters and waitresses already make too much money in tips and, besides, the maids work harder. I am going to propose we give the maids ten cents more.'

"The other guys say, 'That is too much.'

"Then Roy Kelley turns to me and nods his head toward the other hotel men and says, 'I have to have a meeting with my board of directors. Excuse us.'

"He marches them off to the men's room for a private conference.

"A minute later he marches them back in again and says, 'Yeah, they all agree now.'"

A moment silently slipped by.

"There wasn't a time I couldn't call him. Not like business people today. They're too busy. They are in conference. Roy had his desk in the lobby and no matter what it was, he was ready to discuss your problem. You would get your answer right then.

"When he was in that automobile accident and had his temporary hospital room in the Edgewater I put a little notice on our bulletin board saying that no one — absolutely no one — was to bother Roy Kelley. If they had a problem, bring it to me.

"I believe somebody took that notice and gave it to him. He appreciated that.

"Later on, I was having trouble with the union headquarters in San Francisco. They wanted to kick me out. So Roy Kelley said, "Well, let's join up with your Teamsters. I'll recognize the Teamsters. All my employees will recognize the Teamsters.'

"Well, the AFL didn't want to lose all those dues-paying members so we worked it out."

Rutledge shrugs again. His face now serious.

"Once we had to pull a strike at the Reef. I don't remember what the issues were but I knew if Roy Kelley paid, all the others would pay.

"But that's another story. He had a gal working for him, Mildred Courtney, who also became an officer of Local 5. She was elected to the office of union secretary. She was a damn good one.

"I told our members to be ready for a strike and Mildred Courtney said, 'What am I going to do?'

"I said, 'You're going to have to decide what to do.'

"She said, 'I'm going to ask Mrs. Kelley.' So she did, and Mrs. Kelley, as I remember, told her, 'It is your union and you have to go with the union. You do that and I'll cover up for you.'

"Mildred was still concerned. 'Mr. Kelley will be mad.'

"'I'll take care of that,' says Mrs. Kelley.

"At that time Roy Kelley was building different things and Mildred was a key person, he depended on her a lot, and the strike was over in about two days.

"Mildred went back to work.

"Roy Kelley looks at her and says, 'What are you doing here? Go home with the rest of them. You walked off.'

"Mildred was heartbroken.

"I called Roy and told him, 'You can't fire Mildred. She told you she had to go out and Mrs. Kelley told her it was her duty to go.'

"Kelley comes back and says, 'She told me all right but I didn't have to believe her.'

"Anyway, Mrs. Kelley stuck up for her and, of course, she went back to work.

"You know, one of the most redeeming features about Kelley is that he can't hold a grudge. Mildred now runs four of his hotels.

"I learned to make decisions from him. He has an honesty about him that you have to appreciate.

"Henry Kaiser was the same way. In the very beginning after Kaiser came here, I got a call about two in the morning. I was asleep. This voice said, 'I wonder when I could have a little of your time?'

"I said, 'Who is this?'

"The voice said, 'Henry Kaiser.'

"I said, 'Well, I'm glad to talk to you. I am the King of Siam.'

"I thought it was some joker waking me up at two in the morning, just being a smart ass.

"He chuckled a little bit and said, 'Could you come to my office or I will come to your office tomorrow morning. When will it be convenient for you?' Like that. At two in the morning. It *was* Kaiser.

"So I went and talked to him and I asked him, 'What are you doing in Hawaii?'

"He said, 'Well, at Fontana,' — that's where the Kaiser

Steel Mill is — 'they came to the conclusion that I was too old. They had ways of letting me know. So I felt I should leave.'

"So he tells me that he wants to build a hotel and he doesn't know anything about the hotel business and what do I think about this and what do I think about that?

"He told me about his first experience with a union.

"I think he was working on his first big dam project. Grand Coulee? Anyway, this union fellow comes to see him and he wants to take Kaiser's workers and make them union members because people need the union protection.

"Kaiser said, 'I think I am doing a pretty good job of running my business and I don't need you.'

"The union organizer left Kaiser's office.

"Then Kaiser said, 'As he was walking down the road, I noticed that my men, what I thought were my loyal men, were getting on the road and following him.

"'Now,' Kaiser says to me — and this is what I liked about Henry — 'What would you have done?'

"'I don't know. Get ready for a strike,' I answered.

"'You know what I did? I went down the road after the organizer, stopped him, put my arm around his shoulder and told him I thought we should go back to the office. Maybe we could work something out. That's how I learned about unions.'"

Rutledge came back to his current problems.

"This land, the Unity House, the Waikiki Marina Hotel that Roy Kelley helped me build, cost altogether about $6 million. It is all going to be sold. I have an offer now for $42 million.

"I want to set everything up on a permanent basis because I'm not going to be around forever.

"You know last Labor Day there was no Labor Day parade.

"We need scholarships. We need more labor education, more pride."

(In December, 1989 the Unity House and the Waikiki Marina Hotel were sold for $43 million.)

Two National Labor Relations Board rulings had serious effects on the membership of Local 5.

One was centered around the union-owned Waikiki Marina Hotel which, naturally, had Local 5 as its bargaining representative. In 1955, in a Bausch & Lomb Optical Company hearing, the Board ruled that an employer is justified in refusing to bargain with a union that is engaged in a directly competitive business.

As a result of the ruling, the activity of Local 5 was inhibited for a period of several years.

"The Local withdrew from numerous campaigns rather than test the issue because Rutledge, who was president of Local 5, continued to maintain control over the Marina Hotel," according to an NLRB official cited in Bernard Stern's excellent book, "The Aloha Trade," a labor history of Hawaii's hotel industry.*

The second NLRB ruling held that a hotel buyer was not required to assume an existing collective bargaining agreement of the former owner. As a consequence, Local 5 suffered serious losses in membership among its Class B hotels because of the multiple hotel sales, particularly to the Japanese.

In 1986 alone, sixteen hotels in Hawaii were sold. The Coral Reef was sold twice in one day.

By 1986, Local 5 represented less than forty-five percent of all hotel units in Waikiki. An astoundingly low figure when compared to the pioneering success of the union.

Stern's history touches on the unique Kelley/Rutledge friendship:

> *"Although Roy Kelley never lost an opportunity to belabor the union, he maintained an unusual and close personal relationship with Art Rutledge, one that defies all pat formulas on what the proper relationship between a union leader and an employer should be. Kelley claims that he never paid much attention to union negotiations, just going along with what Sheraton and Hilton worked out. Any special*

problems were worked out directly with Art Rutledge."

In a footnote, Stern reports Kelley telling him, "I didn't have anything to do with the union. I just talked to Art." *

In 1980, Art Rutledge lost Local 5 leadership to Richard Tam who moved Local 5 out of Unity House.

Rutledge: "This fellow Tam couldn't handle it. The first thing he did was get into a hassle with Roy Kelley. I think he also said something in front of Richard Kelley about Roy Kelley's integrity. That offended Richard and he got hold of a smart lawyer and they eventually kicked the union out of all their hotels. They weren't afraid of the union and they didn't like the relationship that Tam represented.

"Roy is not an anti-people person, and he isn't anti-union.

"He's not an employer who gets angry and holds a grudge.

"I know Richard Kelley is not a John Bircher. I like Richard and get along with him."

When Rutledge was replaced from Local 5 leadership by Richard Tam, the Kelleys took a more aggressive legal stance and, by 1985, had completely eliminated the union from all Kelley operations.

Art Rutledge was asked about his Teamsters' strike against Trade Wind Transportation Company that Kelley, MacGregor and Allen owned.

The mellow tone left his voice. He no longer chuckled.

"Yeah, that MacGregor. He's an egotistical little bastard. I get along good with him, but you know —?"

He shrugs and continues.

"We did have a strike, but I forget what the hell that strike was all about."

Perhaps money?

"Yeah, but money wasn't the root of the thing. I think it was his goddam arrogant attitude. He's a little guy and it just gave him a feeling of power. He was gonna show me, see. The men were on his side, bus drivers, taxi drivers. They are all chiselers. They want cash. They are with you as long as you give it to them. They'll switch off if you don't.

"We'd have been all right if it hadn't of been for MacGregor. Times have changed, but Bob hasn't. He ought to have half a dozen kids that he can leave his money to. Roy Kelley was a genius in bringing other people into his world and making them a lot of money. Bob MacGregor was one of them."

It was time to revisit MacGregor.

Bob MacGregor: "The Outrigger Waikiki was opening up and we had a couple of run-ins with Mr. Rutledge. See, we were a different corporation and not bound by the Kelley hotel contracts with Local 5. Roy was determined not to have the union in there, and we didn't.

"We paid our Outrigger Waikiki employees wages equal to the union hotel wages. We had profit sharing in addition, and there was a substantial profit.

"Well, the Trade Wind Transportation Company had a contract with Rutledge's Teamsters covering our tour bus drivers and Rutledge and I had a disagreement over our contract. In truth, he really was taking his frustration over the non-unionized Outrigger Waikiki out on our tour company because I was the president of the Outrigger.

"Roy and I talked about it. Mind you, this was in 1967, long before Richard came in.

"Roy said, 'If you want to fight this, go ahead.'

"Well, there were three transportation companies. Gray Line, Yim, and ourselves. We all had the same union contracts.

"Rutledge came in and said he wanted a 55¢-an-hour increase.

"We all said no deal. We can't afford that. So we made an offer. He made a counter offer.

"Finally, the three transportation companies got together and agreed that we were not going to go beyond 35¢ an hour. We shook hands on it.

"The next day I come in and my manager says, 'Have you heard?'

"'Heard what?' I asked.

"'Gray Line and Yim have signed with Rutledge for 49¢ an hour.'

"I thought, 'Oh, hell, we are all alone now.'

"I talked to Roy and Roy said, 'Whatever you want to do, I'm behind you.' Great.

"I thought it over and then went to see Rutledge and I said, 'Okay, you win. I'll sign the contract.'

"Rutledge said, 'Oh, yeah? MacGregor, for you, it's not 49¢. It's 60¢ — for punishment.'

"I called him a son-of-a-bitch. I tore up the contract and told him what he could do with it and threw it on the table in front of his committee.

"The next day I go to work and one of my guys says, 'See that red Mercury across the street?'

"'Yeah.'

"'That's the union muscle.'

"Well, during the strike, I had driven a couple of trips and I got a few off-duty army boys to drive cars ... so it looked like a threat of strong arm tactics.

"So I said to myself, if that is the way they want to play, okay.

"I went to see a good friend who was close to another good friend and pretty soon I had a red Mercury too.

"My buses would start around the island followed by Rutledge's gun car, followed by my gun car. Finally, the federal mediator stepped in. 'Mr. MacGregor,' he said, 'you've turned Waikiki into an armed camp.'

"I said, 'No, I haven't. Rutledge has.'

"The mediator said, 'There must be something that can be done here.'

"I talked to Roy and he said, 'Hold your ground.'

"I remember it was Sunday morning. I was supposed

to play polo that afternoon. I was sitting in the lobby of the Royal Hawaiian Hotel, all by myself, outside the two rooms where the committees were meeting.

"On one side of the lobby in a meeting room was Rutledge and his committee, and on the other side was my committee.

"The federal mediator was shuffling back and forth between the two and sometimes talking to poor old MacGregor who was just sitting there by himself.

"The mediator said, 'Offer him something.'

"I said, 'I'll offer him nothing.'

"Finally, he came out and asked, 'Would you settle for 2¢ above Gray Line?'

"I said, 'Yep.'

"So we had a deal and the strike was over. In the meantime, Rutledge's boys had slashed my tires and busted my windshields but we were happy. The strike was over, the Outrigger was full and that is when we all went on the aerial safari to Africa."

The Outrigger corporation bought the Prince Kuhio Hotel in 1982. Under the sales agreement, all 350 employees were terminated by the former owners. The next morning the new owner, Outrigger Hotels Hawaii, started rehiring. Some 300 employees were rehired. The hotel's bakery department, which had been operating at a tremendous loss, was eliminated. The other Prince Kuhio departments — personnel, payroll, maintenance, reservations — were either trimmed or incorporated into the Outrigger corporate structure.

Local 5 picketed the Prince Kuhio for thirty days, without effect.

By 1985, all of the Kelley hotels were under a single corporate umbrella and operating without a union contract.

The only differences for the 3,000 employees, according to Dr. Kelley, are that the Outrigger's employees, who are paid union scale wages, have a profit-sharing plan instead of a union pension fund.

Tony Rutledge has since gained control of Local 5.

Art Rutledge, in 1989, mellowed but, at age eighty-three, was still sharp, colorful, witty and aggressive.

He says of Roy Kelley, as one street fighter of another, "It has been a privilege knowing him."

---

* Quotes from "The Aloha Trade" are reprinted with permission from copyright owner Janet Stern.

CHAPTER EIGHT

*Tenants, Suppliers, and
Other Decorated Veterans
of the Kelley World*

Richard (Dick) Norstrom is chief executive officer and president of the Outrigger Shops in all Outrigger properties. The company has twelve stores and, at the end of 1989, was doing about $13 million in sales.

Dick is a graduate of the University of Hawaii and the Kelley School of Long Hours.

Tall, tanned, youthful despite a scattering of thinning hair, he has the look of a man of the sea and, indeed, he spends a lot of his off-duty time in his sailboat. A wide, relaxed grin is another characteristic.

As he speaks he places two five-by-eight-inch blank pads and a pencil on the table.

"These are samples of the infamous Roy Kelley scratch pads. And this is a #2 pencil. An architect's pencil. That's all he ever drew with.

"He had a stack of these — about four inches high — always on the right hand corner of his desk in the lobby. Along with a pile of junk, publications and the like.

"There was always a chair at the right side of his desk.

Anybody could come and sit there. Bellboys, maids, retirees. They would have been those who weren't intimidated by him.

"Well, you know he was blind in his left eye so if you came up on his left side you would have to start off by saying something. Otherwise, he wouldn't know you were there.

"Salesmen would come and sit at the desk to sell their products. They had to know everything about what they were selling because Mr. Kelley would interrogate them to the 'nth' degree. I saw some of them leave really embarrassed. He wasn't above calling their bosses and telling them to send someone down who knew what they were talking about.

"One thing about Mr. Kelley — I still call him 'Mr. Kelley' to this day — he had an unsurpassed ability as an ass chewer. He really knew how to do it. Really cut you down if you deserved it. He was like a street fighter. Fearless. He would take on anybody.

"It happened to me a number of times. He would catch me screwing up and I would go home at the end of the day practically in tears. But the beautiful thing was the next day he would talk to me like it never happened.

"My career with Mr. Kelley started off by my marrying a Kelley. I was a paint salesman with Dutch Boy Paints and was about to move to Manila with the International Division when my father died, so I moved back to the family home to be near my mother and enrolled in Santa Rosa Junior College. There I met Pat Kelley and we were married and moved to Hawaii in 1957.

"I went to work for the Kelley hotels to learn the hotel business and started as a utility clerk in the Islander Hotel. We never had the pleasure of being labeled 'desk' clerks. We were 'utility' clerks. That meant we did everything and anything. Like hauling sea trunks up three flights of stairs, which we often did on Saturdays.

"We had a lot of military personnel who would come and stay with us while they waited for housing. We were so cheap. They would come in on what we called 'Boat Day' and we would haul their trunks up to their rooms. The military wasn't great on tipping either.

"I had a passion for getting a college degree in business and I enrolled in the University of Hawaii with a lot of real tough time-consuming courses.

"Well, here I was, married, working at the Islander six days a week from three in the afternoon until eleven at night, going to the university all morning. I couldn't take my school work to the hotel because I worked under a lot of pressure, and it was hard getting all the required studying in.

"One semester I was carrying sixteen units and was still subject to emergency calls to come down to work at the hotel. Like the time the Reef was flooded. Among the casualties of the flood were jillions of pepper mills. They were to go in The Pepper Room, a new dining room in the Reef. So Pat and I had to go down on a Sunday, my day of study. We spent the whole day drying out pepper mills and trying to save the soaked decals on the side.

"I think they were all eventually thrown out but that's where I spent the Sunday before my business law exam on Monday.

"With all of the crazy things that were always happening, I was getting worn out. I had been in Honolulu about a year then and I went to see the hotel manager, a lady named Irene Branch. She had come over to the Islander from the Biltmore Hotel. I told her I was demoralized; it was such an uphill battle. But she couldn't do anything to change my hours.

"I didn't want to leave the hotel. I didn't have time to study, or make a lot of friends, and Pat was saying 'Why don't you spend more time with me?'

"Finally, I got up enough courage to go to Mr. Kelley: 'Hey, could I maybe get my hours cut down, or even go to a five-day week, so I could get a little more rest? I need to do something.'

"Out comes the scratch pad and the #2 pencil.

"'Okay,' he starts, 'how many classes do you take?'

"'Well, I take sixteen units.'

"He says, 'You study two hours for each hour in class.'

"He remembered that used to be the rule of thumb.

"He is jotting figures on his pad throughout our conversation. He goes on, 'You sleep eight hours a day.'

"Then he adds it all up, including time for eating. 'Look here,' he pushes the pad in front of me. 'This shows you have a surplus of between twenty to thirty hours a week. What are you doing with all those hours?'

"Boy, was I flattened. What was I going to say? Nothing. What I learned to do was study in weird places and at weird times.

"Then Pat and I were divorced.

"Mrs. Kelley told me several times how much she and Mr. Kelley liked me and not to worry about it. He still would refer to me as his son-in-law even when Pat's other husband might be in the room."

Dick pauses, his smile temporarily gone as he rethinks the past. A slight gesture brings him back to the future.

"Mr. Kelley showed me how to make a hunk of money without ever taking one penny of credit. It was one of the beautiful ways he helped people. He was masterful in letting me do things for myself, in letting me keep my integrity and individualism, letting it all be my ball game, even though he triggered the action.

"For example, several years went by and I was still working at the hotels. I had a girl friend, Margie. A locally born Japanese. We were going to get married and we had saved our money together.

"She worked in the catering department at the Reef. She also took on a second job as manager of an apartment building for Ed Bauer, Mr. Kelley's architect buddy, and went on night shift for the catering department. Then she also took on the management of Bob Black's apartment building around the corner from the Bauer apartment house and got a free apartment as part of the deal.

"Well, I had free food and rent. We didn't go partying

or bar hopping and, in a period of time, we saved a good amount of money. I kept Mr. Kelley up to date on how much money we had in the savings account.

"One day in December of 1963, I told Mr. Kelley 'You know there is a piece of property up by the Ala Wai Canal that's for sale. This lady has two lots with two small apartment houses on them and I'd like to buy them.'

"Boy, did I get reamed out. 'Don't be so stupid!' he yelled at me.

"'I'm not stupid,' I yelled back. It got very heated and I walked out. I was so upset and very hurt that he talked to me like that.

"I didn't know if my relations with Mr. Kelley were permanently damaged, or what. I couldn't have been more depressed. Okay?

"Now, here it comes. The next day I am coming out of the basement of the Edgewater Hotel where I had dropped off the day's receipts and — oh, my God — there he is, standing across the street. He's been waiting for me.

"He calls me over and he says, 'I want you to go over and see Stanley Gilmore. He owns that property there on the corner. I think he will sell you the property, but don't offer him more than $210,000. You can probably get it for $20,000 down. Don't offer more than seven percent interest on the balance, on an agreement of sale. He'll probably take an agreement of sale.'

"Later on I realized that he had this whole thing wired. He had gone over and seen Stanley earlier that morning, but he didn't tell me that. He wanted me to feel like I was making my own deal.

"So I went over and saw Stanley the same morning and we talked about a few things and then it became obvious that the deal was already set. The price was $210,000 and he would accept $20,000 and seven percent interest on an agreement of sale.

"The deal closed on January 2, 1964. Mr. Kelley loaned me some money. Of course I repaid every last cent.

"There were eighteen apartments in the building we

bought. Margie left the Bauer apartment job and took over management of our own place.

"I would get off work about six or so and we would spend our evenings getting the apartments fixed up. I knew all the guys in the trades who worked for the Kelleys so everything was cost plus. Labor was moonlighting guys. We got the place looking real nice for very little money.

"Our room rate was $35 a week, or whatever we could get. We had one maid and, when she was out, Margie or I did the cleaning.

"Then Mr. Kelley talked to us about operating the Patterson Cottages up on Beachwalk. They were pretty worn out, tired cottages but Mr. Kelley had a lease on the property and we were doing so well with our units that he asked us to take over the Patterson Cottages until he was ready to build on the property. All he wanted out of it was enough to cover the property tax and the lease rent.

"The Patterson Cottages took a lot of cleaning and fixing but we hired another maid and turned them around. We made a lot of money. This went on for four years.

"Then out came the scratch pad again.

"I think it was about noontime. I was standing on the street talking to Guy Marshall, a friend of Mr. Kelley's and later a partner in one of his hotels. Mr. Kelley comes up and he takes out a scratch pad and starts drawing. He drew a basic floor plan with ten units on a floor. He said, 'If you want to build on your property, I think you had better do it now. Start with something like this.'

"Fortunately, I used to walk through a lot of construction projects with him on Sunday afternoons and went through a lot of architectural drawings at the same time.

"In the Waikiki Surf, where I was working, there was a store room. I put a couple of old easy chairs in there, laid a plank across them to make a drafting table. I had a draftsman friend who gave me some tips and I started drawing plans.

"During the seven months I worked on plans for that building, Mr. Kelley would spend anywhere from an hour to three hours on Sunday afternoons in his drafting room going through my rough sheets, coaching me, sometimes scolding unmercifully. Oh, it was tough.

"He put me in touch with a mechanical engineer, and an electrical engineer and a structural engineer by the name of Dick Libby who used to do work for him. I remember Dick Libby's remark, after looking through some of the changes Mr. Kelley had made on my drawings, 'Roy Kelley is the only real genius I ever met.'

"Mr. Kelley used to drive Dick crazy because he wouldn't pay his fees. Even on my building! His fee came to $3,200 and Mr. Kelley calls Dick and says, 'Norstrom's only going to pay you $2,500 because it is not worth $3,200.'

"When it came time for the serious money, Mr. Kelley said 'We're going to meet Cliff Terry for lunch at the Pacific Club.'"

Cliff Terry was the president of the Bank of Hawaii.

"After lunch, we go to Terry's office and Mr. Kelley lays out the drawings and he says, 'Cliff, Norstrom, my son-in-law, drew all of these plans and he needs $500,000 and he can't pay you anything over seven percent.'

"And Cliff Terry says, 'Oh, that's no problem.'

"See what I mean? I am so indebted to him. It's like he is my father. I actually have fun bragging about him.

"So I had the bank money, Stanley subordinated the agreement of sale, and we were set. Ed Bauer came back into the picture and was very helpful in getting the specs out to the contractors. The bids came in. We got a great contractor, Nakakura. The construction cost was $800,000.

"The first major pour was the lobby floor which had a lot of steel in it. The pour was set for Monday morning but on the Friday before, Mr. Kelley called me at the Waikiki Surf and said 'You'd better call your contractor and tell him that they can't pour. The steel is set in wrong.'

"I learned that the trades can make bad mistakes. After that, I made this little wooden instrument that I used to check my steel every Sunday.

"As we got on the higher floors I used to go up on Sundays and look out at the ocean and see the sailboats out there and I would think, 'That is one of the rewards of life. When you get liberated, the symbol is owning a sailboat.'

"I have had a sailboat now for twenty years.

"We did well operating the Kalia Inn and sold it after five years for a price that, at the time, looked great. Not compared to today — but you can't look back."

Dick shrugs and changes the subject.

"Has anyone told you about Mrs. Kelley's Sunday waffles?"

Without waiting for a real answer, he continued.

"They were the best waffles in the world. Sunday morning was Roy Kelley Time and, if you were among the chosen few, you would be invited up to have waffles with him.

"Mrs. Kelley's own recipe. She made them by hand and cooked them in her own waffle iron. I think it was an antique.

"There would be Mr. and Mrs. Kelley, Pat, visitors, who-ever was in town, including salesmen.

"There was another thing that Mr. Kelley taught me and that was loyalty. I practice it today.

"He might get on some salesmen unmercifully but, time and time again, the faithful walked away with fat order books.

"I remember a representative of the Baker Linen Company in Seattle. When he came to town, a Mai Tai drink was waiting for him in his room and an invitation for Sunday waffles.

"Another cute thing. When I was managing the Waikiki Surf, Sunday was my day to be on duty. Well, after Mr. Kelley would have his waffles, he would call whoever was on duty in his hotel and get a room service tray and load it up with whatever looked good — sometimes he would call and ask me what I wanted — and Guy Marshall would drive him over to the Waikiki Surf and give me lunch.

"I would take it into the storeroom and eat, and he and Marshall would go through the traffic sheets, or hand out keys, or sign in guests. Whatever."

Turning to his current position in the organization, Dick Norstrom digs into a different part of his history.

"The root of my retailing interest probably goes back to post-college days. Lots of guys my age talked about going into business for themselves.

"You know the line: 'I'm not going to work for anybody. I want to do my own thing.' That always kind of stayed with me.

"I got the idea that it would be neat to have a liquor store, a classy one with a gourmet shop, that type of thing. Well, Mr. Kelley had a location on a property on Kalakaua Avenue that he said he would rent to me if I could get a liquor license.

"I raised some up-front money and got hold of William Richardson because he was supposed to have the best connection with the Liquor Commission. Richardson's office was in this old building down in Chinatown. I gave him $250 and said I wanted a liquor license.

"I don't think Mr. Kelley was too keen on the idea because I was still working for him as a hotel manager.

"But I went through the whole routine anyway. Richardson called me down to his office to report 'Sorry, the Liquor Commission feels that the area where you want to set up a liquor store is already saturated with liquor stores. Thank you.' He kept the $250 and I left without a license.

"Lots of time goes by and Mr. Kelley gets the Outrigger Canoe Club site and starts working on the plans. He called me over to see him. Anytime Mr. Kelley called, you dropped whatever you were doing. If you couldn't find your keys to your car, you *ran* to his office. That's not an exaggeration. That's the way his company worked.

"He was at his drafting room working on plans for the new Outrigger Waikiki. He had outlined a shop space on the ground floor and said, 'If you're interested, I think that space would make a very good liquor store.'

"See, he remembered all of that time. We never talked about it after I got shot down by the Liquor Commission. But he never forgot it. That's typical of Mr. Kelley."

The easy smile spreads across Dick's face.

"He never signed his name to anything. If he told you he would make a deal with you, you got it. You never had to remind him."

Roy Kelley had returned from Hong Kong where he saw the profitability of stores occupying the ground floor space of hotels. It was another 'first' for a Waikiki hotel, but the Outrigger shops built out to the edge of the sidewalks were not without community criticism. On the other hand, they were very profitable.

"He would care as much about your business and care as much about your having good sales and making money as you would. Often times, he was one step ahead of you. Kind of hurt sometimes. Here he is telling you how to run your business and he knows more about it than you do.

"Mr. Kelley watched over the shops like a mother hen. He was a freak about burned out light bulbs. Or if anything was not square, not straight, you either got it straightened out or he would straighten it out himself.

"We started out paying ten percent of gross sales as rent. Now, its up to twelve percent. His daughter, Jeannie Rolles, keeps tightening the screws. There are no loose ends. We're not favored children by any means.

"I've been talking about Mr. Kelley all of this time but I can't forget Estelle — Mrs. Kelley. She was a very dominant person herself. She was never a 'little old lady in tennis shoes.' She shot from the hip too. Blow you away if you trod on her toes.

"Once a branch manager at the First Hawaiian Bank wouldn't accept a check to me signed by her. Well, she got him on the phone and told him the facts of life. I went back to the bank with the check and he accepted it ... eagerly. Very eagerly.

"When Margie and I set the date to be married, we kept it very quiet. I didn't know how the Kelleys were going to feel about their ex-son-in-law remarrying. Especially a local girl. We got married at the Church of the Crossroads.

"The day of the wedding, the phone rang and it was Mr. Kelley and he says, "I want to wish you all of the best.' Then a little later, Richard calls. Same thing.

"One day, not over a year ago, Mrs. Kelley said to me, 'You know, I always wanted to tell you this but never got around to it. I wanted to tell you that Roy and I felt really badly that we were on a round-the-world trip and couldn't attend your graduation.'

"Thirty years later and she never forgot it.

"She's a wonderful person. They both are."

Al Batz, Concessionaire

Al Batz is a veteran of several original Kelley food and beverage operations and now has the concession for The Brass Rail, a small sandwich-and-beer bar on the ground floor of the Outrigger Waikiki on Kalakaua Avenue.

He is a black-headed Basque, with the features and mannerisms of his countrymen. He is expansive. Exuberant. His hands are expressive, they know only perpetual motion. His French accent, moderated.

"I was born in the south of France in the Pyrenees Mountains. I had just finished the French Hotel School in Dijon and I was going to go to New Orleans with a family. They stopped in Cuba and I stayed there for a while and worked at the Gran Nacional Hotel as a busboy. I liked it. Class place. Gambling and all.

"Then I went by boat from Havana to New Orleans. Worked in first class hotels there.

"Then I was in the war as a paratrooper, 101 Airborne Division.

"After the war I worked in San Francisco. The Fairmont Hotel. The Clift. Then I was hired to come to Honolulu and open the Biltmore Hotel as food and beverage manager. It wasn't my cup of tea for some reason.

"That's when I hooked up with Mr. Kelley. With me, it's not 'Roy,' it's 'Mr. Kelley' — all the time. Always has been.

"Well, I heard he was looking for somebody to run his new dining room in the Reef Hotel.

"I didn't make an appointment but just went over to the

Reef and went up to this guy in a plain shirt and wrinkled pants and white hair seated at a little desk in the lobby and I asked, 'Where is Mr. Kelley's office?'

"He said, 'This is it.'

"I was kind of shocked. I thought Mr. Kelley would have a big office like all the hotel managers I had known.

"'You're Mr. Kelley?' I might have sounded surprised.

"'That's right,' he said. 'What do you want?'

"So I told him that I had heard that he was looking for someone to run his dining room. He wanted to know how much experience I had had. After I got through, he called Bill Kelly — same name but spelled different, no relation. All he said was: 'You'd better hire this guy.'

"Right then and there I was hired. Well, Bill Kelly died not long after that and I was in charge of a big dining room. Banquets and all that. The bars. The Pepper Mill Room. After a while, I thought that maybe I should go into business by myself.

"I didn't have any money. I had just gotten over a divorce. But I heard this guy had a small hotel at Seaside and Kuhio called the Waikiki Surf. He had a little dining room on the corner and I thought if I could get it, fix it up as a little French restaurant, I might make a few dollars. So I did. Called it Le Parisien.

"Well, it went like a house on fire from the very beginning. And it was small. Maybe seated thirty people. But all the big people in town loved it.

"Then Mr. Kelley, he came in and bought the hotel and renamed it The Islander. I told him he bought it just to get me back. 'No,' he said, 'but you can do better than this small room.'

"He gave me the big dining room in the hotel which was all Japanese. I changed it to French decor and added a little room by the pool which I called Le Petit Salon.

"Every Sunday the Kelleys had brunch there. The whole family, Jeannie, all the Kelley kids.

"Then he added on a little bar and the place was doing very well.

"But I wanted to try it on my own once more so I started

a place at McCully and Kalakaua called Le Coq d'Or, another French place.

"'Well, Donald Graham of Dillingham Corporation used to come in to have lunch there all the time. One day he said, 'We are building a revolving restaurant on top of the new Ala Moana Building and we'd like you to operate it.'

"I said I didn't have enough money. He said 'If we give you a lease, you can get the money.'"

The highrise Ala Moana Building was part of the new Ala Moana Center, the largest urban shopping center in the United States when it opened in 1959 with 150 shops and 5,000 parking spaces. Later it had 180 shops and 7,500 parking places.

"That's when I got in with John Felix and his father who supplied the money. Well, the restaurant didn't work and I pulled out and there I was without a job again.

"I went back to Mr. Kelley. 'Do you have a job for me?'

"He said, 'I told you you'd be back.'

"He had just finished building the Outrigger Waikiki so I went in as food and beverage manager, ran the bar, ran the banquets. One man, see, just one man. But Mr. Kelley liked it that way.

"But, hey, I truly like this guy so much. Him and Mrs. Kelley both, because it is just like a Mom and Pop story ... but a BIG Mom and Pop story. He with his little desk in the lobby. She handling all the reservations.

"Then he started leasing out concessions like this one, The Brass Rail. Only then it was called The Mini Pub."

Roy Kelley's approach to Al Batz was, "You are going to run this bar and we are going to be partners. The hotel's going to take twenty-five percent off the top for rent and, after that, everything is yours."

"That was a good move on Mr. Kelley's part because bars and dinning rooms in hotels, especially first class hotels, were not money makers. You got managers to pay and all kinds of ways to lose money here and there.

"But, this way, the guy who has the concession is out to make money. He's going to watch the payroll. He's going to watch his expenses, his buying. He's going to put in long hours because, while he might not pay himself any salary, what's left is his.

"So, Mr. Kelley started doing this in all the bars and dining rooms and it has worked out very well.

"You know he goes around to different hotels to have lunch.

"On Saturdays, he and Mrs. Kelley come here for lunch. I set up a table for eight and if there are going to be more, Mrs. Kelley calls me and tells me to set up a few more chairs.

"He has one cold beer from a frosty mug always waiting for him in the freezer, nice and cold. And his potato chips are waiting. For seven years I have taken only one order from them. They always have the same thing: a combination sandwich with ham, turkey and Swiss cheese. She likes sprouts on hers. He doesn't want sprouts but has onions instead. They only eat half of their sandwiches.

"He comes in first and I bring him his beer and he'll say, 'Sit down.'

"But I don't sit down. If I sit down there, I don't feel comfortable. I hear all these people call him 'Roy' or 'Old Man.' I can't do that. But I love the guy so much. You know why? He likes French people and I was born and raised in France.

"Him and me, we start to talk in French. We sing French songs when there's nobody here. He likes that. The guy is amazing. He knows French songs that I have forgotten.

"I told you I was a paratrooper in World War II? He likes it when I tell him war stories. I jumped in Normandy in the invasion. Because I spoke French, the Counter Intelligence Corps borrowed me from the division to jump ahead of the first wave of troops.

"Our mission was to go to Caen in Normandy and capture the mayor, the chief of police — *collaborateurs*, you know — and the telephone switchboard. Well, we sneak into Caen about one in the morning and we get to the mayor's house, knock on the door, and a woman's voice calls out in French, '*Qui est la?* 'Who is there?'

"I answer in French, '*Madame, nous sommes Americains.*' 'We are Americans.'

"She asks, '*Que desirez vous?*' 'What do you want?'

"I answer in French, '*Nous voulons le maire de ville.*' 'We want the mayor of the town.'

"Well, you know in the south, in the Pyrenees, we don't speak with the rapid Parisian French accent.

"And then we hear her holler to the mayor, '*Tiens! Il y a un Americain dehors qui parle francais avec un accent du Sud.* 'What! There is an American out there who speaks French with a southern accent.'

"Mr. Kelley loved stories like that.

"Then I got two combat jumps in Holland. There was a nice one on a Sunday morning. I got hit twice.

"I think Mr. Kelley likes adventurers. He had a manager of the Davey Jones Locker Bar in one hotel who was an ex-stuntman in the movies. But he was drunk every day and Mr. Kelley finally had to let him go.

"He made me put my 101st airborne insignia up over the bar. There it is, the Screaming Eagle.

"All kinds of people show up for Saturday lunch. They come in one by one. They know they will find Mr. and Mrs. Kelley here on Saturdays. The Doctor comes, his family comes. The president. The vice president. They all come to pay their respects.

"I would like to be like Mr. Kelley. After you get used to dealing with him and his direct ways, it is very hard to deal with corporate people with their memos and computer print-outs and stuff like that. I was brought up on his style.

"We never had no contract. No lease. He said, 'Take that bar over and see what you can do with it.' That was it.

"You know, I average about $20,000 a month. That's $5,000 a month in rent to the hotel. That's not bad.

"But I watch the payroll. I only got one girl in the day and one girl at night. I'm in the kitchen. I do all the sandwiches. I do the buying. Everything. That's why I come out pretty good.

"I should have done this years ago."

Another Concessionaire

Paul Elsnor, now seventy-seven years old and retired "for the last time," is building a home in the middle of a macadamia nut orchard on the Big Island.

His earliest career as a building contractor in Southern California might have been a factor in his thirty-three-year friendship with Roy Kelley. That, and his business acumen.

Paul Elsnor left the building trade at the suggestion of a beauty parlor operator and went to a hair-care school in San Diego for nine months.

He came to Hawaii to work in the Elizabeth Arden Studio in the Royal Hawaiian Hotel and, eventually, took over the shop, renaming in "Paul's."

"In the late Fifties I went over to the Reef Hotel to see Roy Kelley about a rumor I'd heard. That the beauty shop in the Reef Towers was going out of business. I asked if I could buy it and he said sure, go ahead.

"We talked over the lease and he stuck out his hand to seal the deal. 'That's the best I have. If that isn't any good, my signature isn't either.'

"Then he added, 'You are now a member of my Pigeon Club.'

"And I asked, 'What's the Pigeon Club?'

"And he said, 'Anybody who contributes ten percent of their income to me.'

Paul laughs and goes on.

"When he added a new building onto the original Reef, he called me and asked, 'Do you want to put another beauty parlor in there?'

"I said, 'Sure.'

"Then he said, 'You might as well buy the one that is downstairs.'

"So I did. The one downstairs was sort of a quicky but the one upstairs was a first class salon.

"From then on, whenever he built a new hotel he'd call me and say, 'Where do you want your beauty parlor?'

"I was an automatic fixture in Kelley's hotels for about

twenty-five years with five shops. No lease, nothing but a handshake. A member of the Pigeon Club.

"I also got into most of the other major hotels and, eventually, had seventeen shops with a hundred employees and grossed about $1 million a year.

"All of the time I operated the beauty shops, I had my construction office in the back so I was running a construction business as well.

"I built my own shops. I used to go down to the Reef at six in the morning and start working, building my own cabinets. Roy would be down there sweeping water out of the garage.

"The reason he and I got along so well is that I worked from daylight until dark — as he did — seven days a week.

"He was tough. He and I had a few words over the years but they were forgotten the minute they had been said because we were friends and we had confidence in each other.

"One time when he was building a new hotel, he came into my office about five o'clock and said, 'I need your signature.'

"'On what?'

"'I've got to get a building permit and the inspector is standing downstairs and I need a contractor's signature.'

"I said, 'Give me the papers.' I signed off on his building permit for a big hotel on Lewers Road.

"He almost paid me back about ten years ago when I was building a house for myself on the golf course at Princeville. I took the plans over for him to review. He told me I needed an engineer to put a stamp on them. He said, 'I've got a stamp, and I'd stamp them, but I can't find the damn thing.'

"So I had to go downtown and get the plans stamped."

Paul recalled the morning, about six o'clock, Roy was walking a building inspector down the hall and poked his head into his workshop. "I was beating my brains out building new cabinets for a new shop when I heard him say 'There's the best damn carpenter in the islands.'

"Roy Kelley is the greatest guy I think I ever knew. He was fair.

"We did a lot of drawing together, a lot of talking and a lot of coffee drinking. I was kind of a member of the family.

"Yeah, and a Charter Member of the Pigeon Club."

People On The Periphery

Dick Libby is the structural engineer who worked on Dick Norstrom's Kalia Inn project and later on the Outrigger East.

"Once," he recalled, "I went in and sat at his desk at the Reef. We talked about business and other things. I eventually brought up the matter that I hadn't been paid.

"He said, "Well, how much do you want?"

"I said, '$2,000.'

"'Come with me,' beckoning me to follow.

"We went across the street to the Edgewater Hotel and into this back room piled high with papers all over the place. His Japanese bookkeeper came up — incidentally he always called me 'Mr. Libby' — and he said, 'Would you write Mr. Libby a check for $2,000.' Three minutes later I walked out with my money.

"He really had a lot of faith in the people who worked for him. He gave you a job to do and you did it. If you goofed up, you didn't work for him again.

"You know, he used to say that he could build for sixty-four cents what would cost anybody else $1.06. And it was true.

"First, he would save on the architect fees because he was his own architect. He didn't pay any consultants. The electrical sub-contractor and mechanical sub-contractor would hire their own engineers.

"He used to hire workers on an hourly, rather than a job, basis. He wouldn't have a contingency. He saved on overhead. He paid cash to get better buys and save money and also saved on gross income tax.

"So it was six percent here, fifteen percent there, five percent somewhere else. Or ten cents there, a cent-and-a-half here and two cents there. He would rattle off this format in about two minutes and I was convinced he could do it.

"He had this tremendous memory. He could tell you, years later, the construction details in every one of his buildings. What the plumbing was like. How much reinforcing bar was in a building. Everything. And he could recall vividly how the building went up.

"One ingenious architectural angle that I have heard about — but never had confirmed — has to do with the Reef Hotel. He sloped the ground floor of the building from the sidewalk to the beach upward by a fraction of an inch per foot, maybe a sixteenth of an inch, which meant that, at the beach level, there was enough space beneath that floor to house an income-producing coffee shop!

"Amazing man."

And Another

Joe Dacey has been a meat salesman in Waikiki since 1953. Today, he is chairman of A. H. Hansen Sales, a multi-million dollar purveyor of meats and other food products.

"I used to spend two days a week covering my customers in Waikiki. In the early days all the salesmen wore coats and ties but, in Waikiki, I would put on Bermuda shorts and wear long socks and an aloha shirt.

"I never had any trouble getting along with Roy or Estelle. They were both very pleasant with me and we used to have nice talks.

"Roy never did like the restaurant business. He said he was always losing money, or at least he wasn't making any money, on his restaurants.

"He really never liked operating restaurants in his hotels, which is why he started granting concessions to different operators.

"He was the same way with property he owned. Paul Livermore had a very successful restaurant, The Embers, on a piece of land that Roy Kelley owned opposite Fort DeRussy where the Waikiki Post Office is now. But Paul was on a month-to-month lease. Roy wouldn't give him a long-term lease because he didn't want to be stuck with an unprofitable long-term lease if the restaurant failed or went down hill. I think this policy is still in effect today.

"So Paul moved across Kalakaua Avenue to a new location and his customers followed him.

"Roy then launched Buzz Schneider in his successful restaurant, Buzz's Steak House. Buzz used to be a liquor salesman and, prior to going into business for himself, worked part-time at the legendary Canlis' restaurant.

"Then his son-in-law, Chuck Rolles, started a steak house in the new addition of the Edgewater Hotel and it was highly successful.

"Despite all of the money-making restaurants on his properties, Roy Kelley never did fancy operating restaurants under his own management. He just wasn't comfortable with the idea.

"Perhaps there were too many ways that operators could skin an owner. In buying, in bar operations, in kickbacks.

"In Roy Kelley's simplistic style of operation there was only one thing to look at and that was the bottom line. He could work with that."

The Architect Partners

Johnson and Perkins has been a successful Honolulu architectural partnership for many years, each partner respected for his imaginative designs.

The two men have also been long time friends of Roy and Estelle Kelley with whom they, also, were partners in a 251-unit hotel on Kuhio Avenue, the Outrigger Surf.

Both architects have esthetic appearances, share quiet demeanors, and are slightly bemused while reminiscing.

Tommy Perkins: "I went to L.A. High with Roy and Estelle. We didn't know each other in school although, when we were viewing the graduating class picture in our Blue & Gold Yearbook, Roy and I discovered we were standing side by side.

"I went to architectural school at the University of California at Berkeley."

Allen Johnson interjected: "That's where Tommy and I met."

Perkins: "Val Ossipoff brought me down to Hawaii in 1933 where I got a job as a draftsman with Hawaii Planing Mill for $60 a month."

Johnson: "Val was also in our class. I came down to Hawaii three years later and worked for an architect by the name of Claude Stiehl. He was *the* social architect. Dickey, who was Roy Kelley's first employer, knew everybody, but Claude Stiehl was social. Very social. He knew all the local women, society women."

Perkins: "After Hawaii Planing Mill, I went to work for Claude Stiehl until he ran out of jobs so I went to work for Dickey. Roy was running Dickey's office. Roy was a terrific worker. He worked day and night. He never had any cash because he invested everything. But his mind never stopped working on new projects.

"He found out I had $500 and he kept working on deals to get the money out of me. Finally, he came up with a lot on Aloha Drive which cost $1,900 ... that I could buy for $500 down. It took me a year to pay it off. Roy, in turn, had this bunch of cast stone. So, with my lot and his cast stone and a government loan, we built a four-unit apartment house under a fifty-fifty partnership.

"One day I asked him, 'How much would it take to buy you out of the apartment deal?' And he gave me a very good figure.

"You have to understand that Roy knew my inner soul. He knew everything about me. He also knew I didn't have a penny. But I did, you see. I had money from my mother's estate that he didn't know about. Two days before my option time ran out, I bought out his share. He was stunned."

Johnson: "We did everything together. We hiked up all the valleys. We hiked up Mt. Kaala together. Remember Roy boosting the girls up the rope?" He and his partner had momentarily retreated to their youth. "I remember once we went hiking and came back looking like a bunch of bums, but decided to go to a movie right after the hike without getting cleaned up.

"Roy bought the tickets and held them all in his hand. We had to stand in line quite a while waiting to get in. Finally, the door opened and we started in and Roy opened his hand and there was nothing there but confetti! He had been standing there unconsciously tearing up the tickets. He dropped the remains of the tickets in the ushers hand and we walked in."

Perkins: "At the time of a major tidal wave in Hawaii — I think it was 1946 — there had been four lots on Diamond Head for sale and a Hawaiian lady put $9,000 or $10,000 down on a lot, but the tidal wave scared her and she pulled out of the deal. Roy heard about it and said, 'You go down and buy that lot.'"

Johnson: "I sold my little Japanese house up in Manoa. I sold a couple of duplexes."

Perkins: "I sold the apartment house that Roy and I had built together."

Johnson: "So Tommy and I got the money together, bought the lot and, in the end, made a handsome profit, thanks to Roy. He was always doing things for other people."

Perkins: "We did a successful co-op apartment development and we asked Roy if he would be interested in working with us on a second co-op and he said, 'No. Don't get involved with projects you don't own.'

"Then one day he said, 'I've got a lot on Kuhio and I would like to put a hotel on it but I am doing so much work, I can't get to it.'"

Johnson: "He was building the Outrigger East and the Outrigger West at the same time. So the deal was made where we would put up $150,000 each and he put up $300,000 for a fifty-fifty partnership. We would do all the designing and drawings, with Roy looking over our shoulders, of course. He had these crews working on the other hotels and he would shift them around to work on our project when they had the time."

Perkins: "So we contributed a year of architectural work. Roy contributed a lot of labor. We opened what is now the Outrigger Surf in 1973 with 251 units, most of them with kitchenettes. I think the rate was $16, or $18, a night. Now it goes for about $55."

Johnson: "For the first three or four years we lost money. But we didn't pay taxes. Then it turned the corner and we paid off all the debts and it has been free and clear for a long time."

Was it profitable?

Perkins, modestly, "Oh, I think so. It supported us all these years."

CHAPTER NINE

Former Employees ...
Friends and Colleagues ...
Bankers and Beach Bums

Outside the immediate periphery of Roy and Estelle's most active professional years in Hawaii was a host of acquaintances, partners, and short-term employees. People who were not necessarily in the middle of the maelstrom, or not long in the middle.

One such was Bob Herkes, a veteran Big Island legislator, Big Island county councilman, hotel operator, and entrepreneur.

"I learned more from Roy Kelley in a year than I ever learned from one man in my lifetime.

"My first job was as a lifeguard at the Edgewater Hotel swimming pool. Roy Kelley let me earn some extra money during off-duty hours while I was still in the Army.

"Then when I got out of the Army, I went to work for him full time. I did everything. I was a desk clerk, a night clerk; you name it, I did it. I would even get a call in the middle of the night from Mr. Kelley saying that the night auditor had a heart problem, come down and do the night audit. I didn't mind. I was flattered.

"Everything with Roy Kelley was simple and direct.

"I remember at the Reef there was a cigar box behind the desk and when you wanted change you lowered the cigar box through a hole in the floor to the bookkeeper down below who would put the money you required in the box, and you would haul it back up.

"When Mr. Kelley finished the second building of the Edgewater, he told me that we were going to change all the room numbers in the two buildings so they would be compatible.

"I said, 'Okay, Mr. Kelley. I'll inform the switchboard operators and the front desk clerks and the housekeepers so they will be ready when you want to renumber the rooms.'

"'No, no, no,' Mr. Kelley said, 'you don't understand. We are going to do it *now*. In two days the whole thing will straighten itself out.'

"So we did. We got metal numbers and went around and renumbered all the rooms. The result, for the first two days, was chaos. People didn't know where their rooms were. Telephone operators couldn't find the guests. People kept getting the wrong keys to the wrong rooms. It was an outrageous situation.

"Three days later it was all settled down, just as Mr. Kelley predicted. Today, I am probably the only person in the world who remembers there was any problem.

"Roy Kelley taught me that when something has to be done, just go ahead and do it. No conferences, no consultants, no plans on paper. Just go ahead and do it.

"We took reservations for the second building of the Edgewater while it was still being finished. I'd take guests up to the room and there wouldn't be a door on the room or it wouldn't have a shower curtain, but I'd tell them that it would all be in place when they came back from the beach that afternoon. And, of course, it would be.

"Roy Kelley was a brilliant man. He could remember everything there was in each of his buildings, the construction, the type of plumbing, the amount of wiring, the number of feet of poured concrete. Everything. Phenomenal memory."

Bob Hoffman, another former vassal in the Kelley

Kingdom, worked in the Reef Hotel. He left the Kelleys to go to the Naniloa Hotel in Hilo, then transferred into property development with Boise Cascade on the Kohala Coast of the Big Island, and, subsequently, was involved in various real estate developments.

"I started with Roy in 1957 as the assistant manager and then night manager of the Reef Hotel. There were four people in the management quadrant then: Jim Knaefler was the senior guy, then Pinky Nolan, Paul Rice, and myself.

"We weren't so much managers as we were glorified desk clerks. Roy would never let managers have a desk or a chair. He said, if we had a desk or a chair, we would just sit down and then, when a customer appeared, we would be too lazy to stand up."

Bob tells the legendary story of Roy and Estelle leaving the restaurant cigar box filled with cash before departing on a long vacation with the admonition to the manager that if the cigar box became empty, he was to close the restaurant.

Hoffman's conclusion of the story, however, is very different.

According to Hoffman's version, when the Kelleys returned, the restaurant manager had a pile of cigar boxes filled with cash and tied with red ribbons!

"When the Reef was first built, the general manager was Bill Kelly and he wanted a restaurant in the hotel. Roy didn't want any part of a restaurant, but Bill talked him into it and then went out and bought all this expensive stainless steel kitchen stuff, which made Roy madder than hell. He told Bill — very firmly — that he had to be more careful about spending so much money.

"Then, Bill Kelly told him he had purchased an ice-making machine which would save them much time and labor because it made 2,000 ice cubes per hour.

"Roy said, 'How do you know that?'

"Bill said, 'The salesman told me.'

"Roy exploded, 'Of course, he did, you dummy. He would tell you anything to sell you the icemaker.'

"So he made Bill Kelly go down to the basement where the icemaker was and count the hourly production of ice cubes!

"Hysterical...but so like Roy Kelley.

"Then there was an electrician by the name of Johnson who looked like he just came off a Swedish boat. He wore these Oshkosh overalls with the pant legs coming halfway up his ankles. And white socks sticking out above his lumberjack boots. He had a hundred tools hanging from his belt and sticking out of his pockets. He didn't walk, he loped. *Galunk, galunk.* He was a tall Swede, a head taller than Roy Kelley.

"Well, one day Roy Kelley, not in a very good mood for whatever reason, called Johnson over and told him he wanted him to look at a junction box on the sixth floor.

"Johnson wasn't clear about what Roy was talking about and asked him to repeat it.

"Roy just got up from his desk and went around to Johnson and took him by the wrist, right above the hand, and walked him across the lobby to the elevator, like a little kid. He punched the elevator button and the elevator came and as the people came out Roy Kelley says politely, 'Good afternoon. How are you? Nice to see you,' — all the while holding this big Swede's wrist.

"They got into the elevator and went up to the sixth floor, walked down the hall, Roy never letting go of Johnson until he got to the junction box. Then he took Johnson's hand and put it on the junction box and in a slow, deliberate, not too patient, parental voice said: 'Repeat—after—me. This—is—the—junction—box—that—Mr—Kelley—wants—me—to—look—at.'"

Hoffman dissolves into laughter. The incident reminds him of another Kelley characteristic.

"Roy Kelley was always teaching us neatness. Meticulous neatness. He would sometimes walk across the lobby and see a cigarette butt or a burnt match or a scrap of paper and he would pick it up, walk to the nearest employee, take the employee by the hand, turn the palm up and put the debris into the employee's hand, close the fist and walk away without saying a word.

"It was a sense of honor to live up to his standard. If we saw anything on the lobby floor from the front desk, *swish*, we'd be there in a flash to pick it up.

"We rarely had any trouble in the hotel. But one evening I was working the night shift and ....

"But first, let me tell you about the telephone system. We had these old manual telephones and the girls on the switchboard could plug into every public phone in the hotel simultaneously. If every public phone began ringing twice, that was Roy Kelley's signal that his call was ready. He would go to any phone, pick it up and start talking.

"Or, he would pick up a telephone and slam it down once or twice to make the light flash on the switchboard, then command, 'Get me Mildred' and hang up. Mildred Courtney was then the head telephone operator and he had a great deal of respect for her. Then, in less than a minute, the telephone would ring and he would give Mildred his instructions, whatever they might be.

"Okay. Well, this night I am working the night shift. It was early in the shift and Roy was still there when a merchant seaman who had been down in the bar and had had a little too much to drink came through the lobby. He was angry about something. He walked out toward the cottages which were adjacent to the Reef Hotel. We had a set of glass doors on that side to keep the wind from blowing in and this sailor walked to the glass doors, opened them and went out, slamming the doors so hard on his way out that they bounced open again.

"I said, 'Hey, hey, hey!' And I walked over to the doors and closed them and walked back to my post at the desk behind this great big pillar. Mr. Kelley is working on my left.

"I sensed someone standing in front of me and I looked up and here is this great big merchant mariner and he hauled off and socked me in the eye.

"Well, I came around the pillar and tackled this guy — I had been a good high school wrestler — and we grappled back and forth until I finally got the guy pinned down.

"Meanwhile, Mr. Kelley is watching all of this and finally picks up the phone and slams it down once or twice but a new girl on the switchboard didn't know why the light was flashing or who was on the other end. Finally, Mr. Kelley picks up the phone and got the girl on the line and with a very firm voice said, 'Now—take—this —very—slowly. I—want—you—to—get—Mildred—on—the—phone. Actually—take—Mildred—and—put—her—on—the—phone.'

"Meanwhile, I am struggling with this giant and I was hoping he would hurry up and get the police there.

"The only police officer who worked the Waikiki beat was Chris Feria who was usually on the night shift. We got to know him pretty well. Chris finally came and took this drunken sailor away.

"By now my eye was beginning to puff up and I thought, 'Boy, I am going to get a break tonight. Roy will send me home to take care of this eye.' You see, Kelley worked his managers six days a week and, if we could get a little extra time off, it was glorious.

"Roy Kelley looked at me and said, 'That eye looks pretty bad.'

"And I thought, 'Oh, yes, he *is* going to send me home.'

"He said, 'Why don't you go over to the kitchen and put some ice on that eye and be back in five minutes. I'll watch the desk for you.'

"So that's what I do. I come back with this ice pack in a napkin and he looks at me and says, 'You'll be all right.' He pats me on the shoulder and goes home and goes to bed.

"He was that kind of a guy. There was no such thing as a frantic situation."

Bob unconsciously touches his right eye before continuing.

"While we are talking about security, let me tell you about Herman, our security officer. Herman was six-foot-one and had a black belt in judo. He had hands like a boxer's and was very careful not to hit anybody.

"Between Herman and Chris Feria we didn't have too many problems. Herman used to carry these long six-cell flashlights. We would buy half a dozen of these flashlights at a time.

"Not too frequently he would find somebody resisting arrest, and he would just *bonk* them over the head with his flashlight, bending it all out of shape. Then he would come to one of us and request a new one.

"Chris, just after World War II, was a member of the Metro Squad. These guys went around in aloha shirts and sort of took the law into their own hands. Harry Meyer said if you were seen leaving a bar in the hands of the Metro Squad at one a.m. the chances were that you would never be seen again.

"Well, when Chris would pick up some guy who had been making trouble, he would bring him to the front desk and question him. Then he would take me in back and ask, 'What do you want me to do with him? Book him or just scare him a little bit?'

"Usually, we would ask Chris just to convince the nut that he shouldn't come around our hotels anymore. Chris would take the guy down to the basement where his sins and omissions would be pointed out to him in one fashion or another and then they would drive off. Last time that guy would come on our property.

"Security was no problem. But overbooking was.

"Not long ago, Richard Kelley was telling a group of us about a truck stop accommodation the Outrigger Lodging Services has in New Mexico that runs one-hundred-and-two percent occupancy.

"I turned to the person next to me and said, 'Hey, that ain't no big deal. We used to do that at the Reef Hotel every day.'

"Qantas Airways flight crews, for example, used to come in and we would give them a day rate. They would shower, take a nap, we would give them a call and they would be gone. We'd clean up the room and rent it again.

"And Bob Herkes! He would convince people going to

the Neighbor Islands that rooms might not be available when they came back to Oahu. The ocean-front room, double, only cost $10 or $12 a day, and he would tell them, 'You can leave your extra luggage in the room and we'll take care of everything and your room will be all ready when you come back.'

"That sounded like a good deal. They would buy the idea and, as soon as they left, he would take the luggage out and store it, rent the room, and then put the luggage back into the room — right where it had been — just before they came back from the Neighbor Islands.

"One time, when we were badly overbooked, we filled the banquet room across the patio from the main desk at the Reef with every box springs and mattress out of the basement.

"We didn't put the mattresses on top of the box spring. Oh, no. We split them and made two beds and charged $5 each a night.

"You know about Estelle's reservation system? No reservations were taken when the yellow tabs got more than three knuckles high? Well, that didn't protect the hotel from people staying over or a flight being cancelled. So we had overbooking, despite her system.

"My son is in the hotel business and overbooking means, according to his terminology today, you have to 'walk' the guest. We used to call it 'shafting.'

"More often than not, it fell on the shoulders of the night desk manager to do the shafting. Over a period of time you become a walking psychologist. I could stand at the top of the stairs and tell who among the arriving guests we could shaft and who we couldn't.

"The guests who hadn't made a deposit or hadn't reconfirmed. They were the easy ones. They got shafted. Then there were the guests who knew their rights and wouldn't put up with being shafted. You could spot them all.

"But you'd get some poor little soul who was en route to wherever and he was only going to be there one night and we would say, 'Oh, yes, we have your room ready in our Reef Annex right down the street.' And we'd call Charlie Ho or Ronnie

Ho and say, 'Take Mr. Smith down to the Reef Annex.'

"They would say, 'Oh, yes, of course. Come with me, Mr. Smith.' And they would load him into a car and drive him down to the Breakers or the Hawaiiana. We would have called ahead to tell the hotel that one of our guests was coming down to 'our' Annex.

"Sometimes, the one we had to shaft and the one we had to take care of would come in together. So we would say to the one we had to shaft, 'Your room is not quite ready. Why don't you go down to the bar and see Eddie and he'll fix you up with a complimentary Mai Tai while we get everything straightened out.'

"And we'd call Eddie Kunioshi, the head bartender, and tell him to take special care of these guests. Then we'd get the other guests out of the lobby and to their rooms and by the time the to-be-shafted guests came back from the bar, they were feeling mellow and pliable. Not too difficult to shaft.

"One thing we couldn't ever do was to be uppity with a guest. Kelley would get all over us.

"On the other hand, if a guy was really, really obnoxious and really needed to be told off, Kelley's instructions were to 'Call Pinky and both of you get together and chew the guest out and get it out of your systems. You'll both feel better. But you have to understand one thing, I'm the final judge of whether or not you exercised good judgment.'

"He was a funny guy. Once, while he was still in his wheelchair after the accident, he came into the lobby while Pinky was banging on the front desk bell, calling for a bellboy to take care of an old lady standing there. No one showed up, which incensed Roy and he grabbed the lady's bag, put it on his lap and wheeled toward the elevator saying, 'Follow me, lady.'

"Another time he was at a Hawaii Hotel Association meeting and someone wanted to know where Chuck Rolles, his son-in-law, was.

"Chuck was up in Aspen, Colorado, skiing and opening a new restaurant and Roy answers, 'Oh, he is up to his snow in Aspen.'"

Classmates' Memories

The Outrigger Hotels' annual summer employment policy of hiring some students in a "Summer Fun" program probably had its genesis in the Kelley kids' college custom of bringing classmates home to spend the summer working in the Kelley hotels.

One of the early classmate interns was Bob Berglund, a Stanford graduate with Richard Kelley. Today, he resides in Saratoga, California, and manages the advanced nuclear technology organization for General Electric in San Jose, the heart of the Silicon Valley.

He was interviewed by telephone.

Berglund: "Rich Kelley and I were in Encina Hall together at Stanford as freshmen. We were not exactly roommates but our two rooms had a common entry hallway. Our two rooms actually made a little separate unit. After becoming acquainted during our freshman year, we both pledged the same fraternity, Phi Kappa Sigma, so we shared the same frat house as well.

"Rich extended an invitation to myself and another classmate, Dick Scruggs, to go over to Hawaii and spend the summer working in his family's hotels.

"We spent the summer at their home on Diamond Head.

"Well, the lifeguard was leaving so I got that job. Dick Scruggs was in engineering, so he worked on the construction of the new wing of the Edgewater.

"It was a memorable summer for me in lots of ways.

"I think I was surprised that I was working seven days a week. But, in Kelley hotels, employees worked seven days a week. Mr. Kelley convinced me that was the right thing to do. He was very convincing.

"The normal custom was for all of us, all together, at the end of the work day, to pick up dinner on a tray from the hotel kitchen and drive home.

"That's what happened the night of the accident.

"We had picked up dinner. I got in the back seat of the first car with the dinner tray sitting on the seat beside me. Rich was driving and Roy was in the right front seat. I was sitting right behind Roy.

"Just as you turn onto Diamond Head Road at the end of the park there is an ess curve. Some sailors in another car coming down the hill missed the curve — they had been drinking — and they came off the curb and hit us head on.

"The Kelley car was a four-door sedan. I remember that because I stepped out of the car from the right front door. I hit the seat in front of me so hard that I pushed it forward, and I'm sure that's what broke Mr. Kelley's leg. The seat just broke off the mounts, trapping his leg.

"I wasn't hurt except for a scraped toe. In summertime Hawaii, you know, we didn't wear shoes.

"Another reason that it was a memorable summer was because of Mickey. The three of us — typical guys — were always looking for young ladies. There was an organization called Howard Tours that used to bring co-eds to the University of Hawaii to attend summer classes. The young ladies were housed at Mid-Pacific Institute or the YWCA's Fern Hall.

"At the beginning of summer they always had a 'mixer,' a social gathering to introduce the students to the young officers from Pearl Harbor and Kaneohe Marine bases. Of course, some of the local fellows like us also attended. The gals came from all over North America, and I married one of those girls three years later. Her name was Michelle, or 'Mickey.' She was from Calgary, Canada, but was going to school in Missouri.

"So I had a movie script summer. Lifeguard in Hawaii. Romance under a palm tree. The perfect girl. Married her. Lived happily ever after.

"Roy Kelley, before the accident, was working on drawings for the new Reef Hotel in a drafting room he had in the basement of the Edgewater Hotel. I used to talk to him about the new hotel and about his dreams and the plans he had. It was pretty educational for a kid in college to talk to a person with his mind and his ability.

"Through Mr. Kelley's contacts, he arranged for us to

take a trip at the end of summer to the other islands. We went deer hunting at a friend's ranch on Molokai. We went to Maui and spent a day seeing the sights. Then we flew to Kona and stayed at the Kona Inn, which was the only place to stay in those days.

"He had arranged for us to go fishing the next day but there was a conflict because the same boat had been chartered by a group of Hollywood people to scout for underwater sets to be used in a movie called "Underwater" starring Jane Russell.

"We agreed to double up and we spent a day with them snorkeling and skin diving, looking at arches and caves they later used for filming.

"I got paid for lifeguarding. I didn't come home with much money but I sure had a great summer.

"After graduation, I went into the Navy and became a pilot. We were stationed in Guam but we flew our planes back to Hawaii every so often for maintenance.

"I remember one night I came in with my crew from the aircraft and we were looking for a place to stay. I called Roy or Estelle — I can't remember which — and they put us up in one of their penthouses.

"Brought in rollaway beds and put us up for the night.

"Their hospitality never stopped."

Richard also invited classmates from Harvard Medical School.

One summer visitor was Dr. Robert Burkhardt, now a plastic surgeon in Tucson, Arizona.

Burkhardt: "Rich and I had been in Stanford together and so was Jane, his girl friend, who was to become his wife.

"I didn't know them at Stanford but we started medical school at Harvard together in 1955.

"We were often mistaken for each other because we looked a lot alike.

"Rich and Jane were married after graduating from Stanford and they were among the few married couples in our freshman class. They lived just like the rest of us. I had no idea he was at all well-to-do.

"I used to study with Rich because he and I both studied in about the same manner. Rich always worked very hard. He was a dedicated student.

"Later he and Jane had a baby and I would baby-sit for them.

"One night they came back from a movie and he said, 'Look, why don't you come visit us this summer?'

"I didn't even know where he lived at the time.

"I said, 'Okay. Where do you live?'

"He said, 'Hawaii.'

"'Oh,' I said, 'that's interesting. I've never been to Hawaii.' So, I went out there with another classmate of ours, Richard Sanderson, who also now lives here in Tucson. So, we went over there together and stayed with Roy and Estelle. It was a fascinating experience.

"I didn't work. Sanderson took a job with the hotel.

"We lived in the beach house on the side of Diamond Head. There was an old car, I think it belonged to Jane, which we used but I got in late and slept late so I usually found myself hitchhiking into Waikiki.

"We had dinners together and had a lot of good fun around the family table.

"At the end of summer we went fishing over at Kona. Dick Sanderson had his turn at the fishing pole but decided he didn't want it anymore and gave it to me. I sat down and in about five minutes a giant marlin hit. I got the fish in and it weighed three-hundred-and-forty pounds. I still have the picture.

"One tragic thing happened many years later. Jane had become an avid amateur pilot. She came to Tucson for an air show. At the time, she had some sort of virus. She collapsed during the air show and died. Rich came and stayed with us in our home for about ten days. It was such a tragic thing."

The long distance telephone line was silent for a long minute. When Bob came back on the line, it was with an upbeat voice.

"One occasion I'll never forget.

"Judy, my wife, and I went over to Hawaii a number of years ago and Rich asked us if we would like to attend one of the hotel's business conferences. To Richard, a business conference meant meeting with his father.

"We said, 'Sure. Yes.'

"So we went out with Rich and Roy and the Chinese bookkeeper who has been with them since the birth of Christ.

"We went to a little Chinese restaurant with formica table tops. Not what you'd call the plushest place in the world.

"So they had a business meeting with Rich giving his dad a report on how the hotels were doing and where the money was and ... all of sudden there was a pause. Silence. Rich and his dad looked at each other and they both exclaimed, nearly together, 'Hey, what happened to the other $8 million?'

"I looked down at my plate. I hadn't ordered that much food so it wasn't my fault.

"Well, they gazed at each other for a few minutes and then Rich snapped his fingers and said, 'Oh, the buses!'

"Roy then said, 'That's it. The buses.'

"Eight million dollars? Judy and I are sitting there with our pupils dilated listening to this whole business meeting over a plate of chop suey in a very ordinary Chinese restaurant. Fascinating.

"Estelle was always very gracious to Judy and me. She took us up to her penthouse where she had this very nice fishpond for lovely *koi,* the prized Japanese goldfish.

"She told us how, from time to time, chlorine pills wound up in the fishpond, killing her *koi.*

"She was madder than hell about it but didn't know what to do so, I guess, she had private investigators stake out the place.

"Finally, they figured out what was happening. A kid in a neighboring building that was taller than the Kelley building was throwing chlorine tablets out of his window into her fishpond, killing her prized — and expensive — fish.

"I asked her, 'How do you take care of something like that? Obviously, it had to be a very sticky situation to deal with through regular legal channels.'

"She said she got the biggest bodyguard in Honolulu to go up to the kid's apartment, knock on the door, walk in and confront the kid, and say, 'DON'T—DO—THAT—ANY—MORE!'

"Didn't have any trouble after that."

D r. Richard Sanderson, now a distinguished cardiac surgeon in Tucson, was the other Kelley college guest during that summer.

The common denominator, listening to the three former classmates, was their happy enthusiasm of remembering summer days in Hawaii. It was almost like hearing them recapture the unfettered, carefree spirit of their youth.

Dick Sanderson: "Richard told me he had a job lined up for me with his father in the car rental business. So that summer I worked for Roy Kelley and Bob MacGregor in the basement of the Reef Hotel for the Trade Wind U-Drive Company.

"There was a need to reorganize the financing and the scheduling of cars. I had two or three phones, a little Filipino guy working the cars and two brothers, Ronald and Donald Ho, washing and servicing and cleaning them.

"I had forty-six cars and, in my summer period, we made $12,000. The year before, Mr. Kelley told me, they had had sixty-four cars and had made $8,000.

"I lived with the Kelleys at the house on Diamond Head.

"I worked in the basement but upstairs was a gal by the name of Polly Reeder, a pretty blond who worked on the Mac-Gregor Trade Wind Tours desk. She worked with Grace Wong, a real character. She liked to flash – and shock people with – this oversized pen inscribed on one side with 'Grace Wong's Whore House,' and on the other with 'Green Stamps on Wednesdays.'

"Polly was something special and I used to spend a lot of time upstairs.

"And there was a gal over at the Edgewater by the name of Peggy Hatori who could riffle through a stack of bills and give you an instant accurate count of them. Faster than anybody I have ever seen count bills.

"She was like a gambler with a poker stake. *Zip-riffle-zip*, and she would say, 'That's one hundred dollars.' One time I challenged her and counted out the bills, one by one. One hundred dollars, on the nose.

"Mrs. Kelley used to give us a ride down to the hotel in her old red Oldsmobile convertible every day.

"She was a wonderful, gracious lady. I'll always have a fond place in my heart for her.

"I remember one improbable conversation with her. We were driving to work one day and she said, 'Dick, hand me some Kleenex out of the *puka* there.'

"'Out of the *what*, Ma'am?' I asked.

"She repeated, 'Out of the *puka*.'

"I said, 'I don't know what a *puka* is. I know a *puka* shell has a little hole in it.'

"She said, 'Well, *puka* can mean lots of things. It can even mean a love compartment but, in this case, it means the glove compartment. Now hand me the Kleenex.'

"I nearly fell out of the car.

"I used to work hard for Mr. Kelley — twelve, fourteen hours a day — and take work home.

"Sundays we had off. Saturday nights, Rich would bring home a big filet mignon from the hotel kitchen and we would cut it up and have steaks on Saturday night. I remember that because, on Sundays, we had steak sandwiches from the left-overs.

"Then Sundays, Rich always arranged for us to do different things around the islands. We would go ti-leaf sliding or go surfing on a huge two hundred-pound surfboard he had.

"One time we went to a party given by Ed Kenney, the star of 'Flower Drum Song' on Broadway.

"Another time we went to a Chinese wedding.

"I could never forget Roy Kelley. He had a mind like a steel trap. Nothing got out of it. He would know things as simple as where the soap for the little Japanese ladies came from and where it was stored. He had systems.

"For example, one of his most impressive systems was, if we were walking around the hotel and he wanted to talk to someone, he would stop at any telephone and say to the operator, 'Get me Bob MacGregor.' We'd continue walking around the hotel and then a telephone would ring twice. Roy Kelley would pick up the phone and say, 'Hello, Bob—.'

"He knew the hotel operator wouldn't dare put anybody else on the line except the person he wanted.

"He wore these big thick glasses but nothing got by the guy. He knew exactly what was going on. The small jobs with small people and the big jobs with big people.

"Occasionally, I would work with Jack Gillette, the social director, during Boat Day.

"When the Matson boats like the *Lurline* would come in, we would go out of Honolulu harbor on a little tug boat. The ships from the Mainland would stand off Waikiki and we could come aboard and set up little booths on deck with orchid leis for our guests. We would pre-register them. And anybody else we could grab for the hotel.

"It was a great opportunity for single guys because we saw the best-looking girls first and could line up dates for a week.

"I got tanned very quickly so the girls thought I was a real Hawaiian when I put leis around their necks and said, 'Aloha. Welcome to Hawaii.' Oh, it worked like magic.

"At the end of the summer we went over to Kona and went marlin fishing with George Parker, captain of the *Mona H* fishing boat. Bob was in the fighting chair and hooked on to a marlin that was ten-feet long and weighed three-hundred-and-forty-five pounds.

"Well, Polly and I got married later on and had four children.

"We came back a number of years later and house sat for Jeannie Rolles up in Waialae Iki. We also went back to Kona and watched the fishing boats come in one day and here comes

George Parker on the *Mona H* with a fish on board of the exact dimensions as that fish Bob had landed!"

Friends And Colleagues

A man of Roy Kelley's individualistic character attracted a host of memorable incidents. Everybody in or near the tourist trade has a "Roy Kelley story."

Harry Meyer, for twenty years owner/operator of the Hawaiiana Hotel, on the same street as the Edgewater, has many.

"I met Roy Kelley because I used to be outside my hotel sweeping the sidewalks on my street at five-thirty in the morning. Roy would come down for his swim about six o'clock and there I would be, cleaning the whole street. Not just in front of the Hawaiiana, but all the way down to the corner.

"The fact that I was crazy enough to sweep somebody else's sidewalk impressed him so much that he offered me a job.

"That's where our friendship began.

"I used to go down and have breakfast with Roy Kelley a couple of times a week. I'd ask him questions. He'd tell me what to do. And I'd do it.

"The best piece of advice he gave me — and remember this is in 1955 and '56 and '57 — was when I inquired about building something and he said, 'Keep building. Buy everything you can. Build everything you can.'

"He loved jokes. If you had a new joke, you always had to take it to breakfast or lunch.

"Anybody could come up to him wanting a room and he'd just say, 'You just go and see Estelle. She'll get you a room.' Estelle really held that thing together.

"One of my favorite Roy Kelley stories is about the time he and Estelle were going on a lengthy vacation. They were going around the world.

"Well, there were about fifty people at the Reef for a going-away party and we were there for about an hour and the time was coming up when they would have to leave to catch the airplane which would connect them with their cruise ship. But there was no Roy Kelley.

"Estelle came over to me and said, 'Harry, can you find Roy?'

"I said, 'I'm sure I can.'

"I knew where he was because when I parked my car in the basement, I saw a maintenance guy working on a sump pump and it was obvious that he was having problems with it.

"I went upstairs and joined the party but I knew, sooner or later, Roy would hear about the trouble with the sump pump.

"I went back down into the basement and there was Roy, still in his travel suit, coat still on, fixing the pump.

"So I bring him back upstairs to the party, his hands covered with grease and dirt. Estelle was beside herself. He tried to wash off the grit — unsuccessfully — said good-bye to everybody and left for the airport.

"You know he had a great talent for building a hotel and having people living in it while it was still under construction. He would finish the ground floor, paint it and rent it, while up above, they would still be painting and jackhammering and everything else and as fast as they would finish a floor, he would have it full. He would have a hotel a hundred-percent occupied long before it was a hundred-percent completed."

Chuck Rolles was an undergraduate at the Cornell Hotel School where he met and dated Jeannie Kelley.

He speaks slowly, this athletically-built, low-key blond who, despite his five-feet-six-inch height, was a famous basketball player. In high school he scored sixty-three points in one game. At Cornell University, he scored forty-two points in one game against Syracuse. During his senior year he averaged twenty-three points a game, still a school record.

During tryouts for the Olympic basketball team, his roommate was Bill Russell who stood six feet, ten inches. It is said they made quite a pair.

One summer, Chuck and a classmate, Chuck Feeney, decided they would like to come to Hawaii and work.

"We wrote to former Cornell people in Hawaii and the word we got back was that Roy Kelley was expanding and building and had lots of jobs.

"We did write to Roy but it was through Jeannie's help that we got jobs.

"When Roy Kelley built the first half of the Edgewater, he had to provide parking so he tore down a bunch of little cottages across the street. All but one, where an old guy living in this cottage had appealed to Roy, 'I am too old to move. I want to die here. Please don't tear it down.' So Roy left it. Tore everything else down and made a parking lot. Well, the old man had died by the time we had arrived and the cottage was being used as a storeroom but we shoved everything aside and moved in there for the summer and went to work.

"I did the night transcript and Chuck Feeney worked as a desk clerk at the Edgewater.

"Phase one of the Reef Hotel opened that summer of 1955 and Roy Kelley was selling rooms for six dollars a day just to get bodies in there and get a cash flow going.

"During one period Chuck and I would be uncrating mattresses and chairs on the lanais and taking them through the sliding windows into rooms and setting them up while Pinky Nolan, the manager, would be in the hallway talking to incoming guests about Hawaii — stalling them really — until we would knock on our side of the door which was the signal that the room was ready, and we would slip out the window. That's how close things were figured.

"At the Edgewater, if a bellboy wasn't there, Roy Kelley would take the bags up to the rooms and people would try to give him a dime or something and he would say, 'Oh, no. Keep it. I own the building.'

"I just have a great deal of love for him. He's a great man.

"One time Roy and I were out in front of the Reef Hotel by the swimming pool where there was a plumbing problem with a water pipe about five or six inches in diameter.

"Roy called in Masuda, his plumber, who had been with him forever and said, 'Masuda-san, we have to take this pipe here, take it here and bend it around this corner, bend it again and make it go back around and down. Do you understand the problem?'

"Masuda said okay and Roy walked away with me and said, 'I don't know if it can be done but, if it can be done, Masuda will do it.'

"We came back the next day and it was done."

The following year, Chuck Rolles graduated from Cornell and he and Jeannie Kelley were married in March. She walked out of her junior year to get married but returned seventeen years later to get her degree.

Chuck Feeney, after graduation, went on to start Duty Free Shops which, today, is an international multi-billion dollar organization.

Bill Wood, editor of Hawaii Investor, is a long time observer of Hawaii's economic scene.

"I think the most amusing story I know about Roy Kelley was that Hung Wo Ching hired him to design the first house that Hung Wo ever built. It was on Kapiolani, down around Date Street, about 1938.

"In those days Hung Wo was a real estate operator."

Later, Hung Wo became one of Honolulu's wealthiest citizens dealing in real estate, cemeteries and an interisland airline. At one time he was also a trustee of the huge Bishop Estate.

"Well, he and Roy Kelley discussed what Hung Wo wanted and they had an agreement. Roy kind of hung back when it came time to leave and, finally, he asked Hung Wo if he wouldn't mind paying him his fee in advance.

"So Hung Wo said sure, and wrote him a check.

"When you realize the millions that Roy Kelley was to be worth later on, it's very amusing."

Hung Wo Ching remembers that first house: "It had three bedrooms and two bathrooms and hardwood floors. I think it cost $8,000 and Roy Kelley's fee was $400, which I paid in advance.

"I got him other jobs and also got those paid in advance.

"Over the years I sold him several pieces of real estate.

"One property was on Ala Wai Boulevard facing the canal. He bought the lot with Charley Parrent who was with Kamehameha Schools. Actually, there were two lots and he paid $1.15 a square foot. He invited me to become a partner in the apartments he was going to build on the lots but I said no because I knew he was going to borrow every dollar he could with a very small equity investment and I was interested, at that time, in going to China and going to school.

"Well, he bought the lots and then he came back to me complaining that there were fishing boats on the property and what was I going to do about them.

"I said, 'I'm not telling you.' A man named Shay had bought these old attack boats from the Navy and stored them on the property. I called Shay and left messages to get rid of the boats. Nothing happened and nothing happened.

"Finally, what happened was the boats were destroyed by a fire.

"Roy Kelley called me after it was all over and thanked me.

"One deal we really missed was the International Market Place. I named it. There was a famous restaurant there, Don The Beachcomber. One night I wanted to take Roy and Henry Kaiser to dinner and we got turned down for a reservation so Roy talked to Don, who I didn't know, and said, 'Either you give us a reservation or you won't get your lease renewed when we take over the property.'

"We got front row seats."

"At one time he offered to sell me the Edgewater Hotel and the newspapers picked it up and ran a headline saying Hung Wo Ching was buying the Edgewater Hotel for $1.3 million. I thought that was very funny because I didn't have anything like $1.3 million.

"I always admired him because he was always such a hard worker. I used to laugh at him because, here he was with one bad leg and one eye, and people would come into his hotel and he would carry their bags to their rooms.

"And when the military would come in looking for a room and couldn't pay the rack rate, he would ask them how much they could pay and that would be the room rate.

"After I had started in the cemetery business I also got involved in buying Waikiki waterfront property near the present Reef Hotel, the same two properties Roy Kelley was interested in, a Damon Estate parcel and the Robinson Estate property.

"Then I got a call from Roy Kelley and he said, "Hung Wo, we make a deal. You handle the dead people. I handle the living.""

Hung Wo gives a fond, high cackling laugh at the story.

The Hotel Association

Bob Rinker was the first paid executive vice president of the Hawaii Hotel Association from 1967 to 1973 and had been an associate of Pinky Nolan in a hotel in Kailua.

Pinky Nolan was an early manager of the Reef Hotel.

"Pinky told me many lovely Roy Kelley hotel stories but, first, I have to tell you about two hotel industry incidents that I knew about personally, because of my position.

"These two stories, I think, personify Roy Kelley.

"When the Hawaii Hotel Association reached a stage of maturity where it needed proper offices, the headquarters moved into the Waikiki Business Plaza. Without saying anything to anybody, it was Roy Kelley who worked out a favorable rental with Bill Mau, the owner of the building, and it was Roy Kelley who put the furniture in the offices.

"Another time, the industry became involved in political campaigns, fighting Mayor Frank Fasi. We collected money and gave it to his opponents. At the end of the campaign, which Fasi won, he and his prosecutor, Larry Chung, ordered a grand jury investigation. Because I was the executive vice president of

HHA, I ended up being indicted.

"It went on a long time, and it wasn't funny. Finally, the circuit court threw the whole thing out. After it was all over, Genie Pitchford, the HHA secretary, told me that Roy Kelley had telephoned her and said, 'If there is anything you need, any resources, let me know.'

"Pinky told me a marvelous story about the time they were building the addition of the Reef Hotel. Construction was up to five floors and was not going as fast as Roy liked, so he was up there inspecting the operation.

"He watched impatiently as a little Filipino guy with a wheelbarrow full of concrete was going along slowly and patiently in his own style from there to here and back again. Roy watched this until he couldn't stand it anymore.

"He takes the wheelbarrow from the laborer and says, 'No. Like this.' And with his bad leg hustles the wheelbarrow from here to there and back again and turns to the Filipino workman and says, 'Now, you got that?'

"And the little Filipino says, 'Yeah, but, Boss, you do that one or two times. I got to do that all day long.'

"And then there was a character named Finklestein who was just a clerk at the Reef. He told Pinky, 'My career is upside-down. I retired from the Army after twenty years and went to work for Roy Kelley. I should have done it the other way. Worked twenty years for Roy Kelley and retired to the Army.'"

Bob claps his hands in appreciation at the line.

"When the IRS came to do an audit, Roy said, 'Okay. The records are all down in the basement of the Edgewater.'

"Well, the agent goes down into the cellar of the Edgewater and there are records all piled into row after row of apple boxes. He fumbles around there for two or three months and finally says to hell with it.

"Pinky maintains that, as a result of that, the IRS regulations were changed saying you had to have an orderly filing system."

Rinker relates another Nolan story that goes back to the

time of a big flood in Waikiki when the Reef cellar was filled with water. The telephone exchange was situated in the basement and the equipment was damaged.

"Well, the telephone company had to send a crew in there to clean up and they must have worked over a week around the clock getting all the parts dried out and back into working order. When they finished, the telephone company sent Roy Kelley a bill for all the work.

"According to Pinky, he sent it right back saying the bill was unacceptable. "It's your equipment and it's your responsibility to maintain it," was Roy Kelley's pragmatic rationale.

"Another time the Feds came in and tried to build a case of hotel collusion on rates. Yeah, the 'Martini Club.' They called everybody in the industry to testify. Everybody but Roy Kelley. I think they came to the conclusion if they put this guy on the stand — this operator who was underselling everybody in Waikiki — he would completely destroy their case.

"I first met the Kelley family when they were vacationing at Mt. Rainier where my wife and I were working. My wife waited on them in the Mt. Rainier Paradise Inn dining room. Her maiden name was Lydgate and he remembered that and whenever he saw her here, he always called her the Lydgate Girl. His memory was like a bloody computer."

The Waikiki Banker

Larry Johnson, son of a popular dermatologist, Dr. Howard "Skin" Johnson, became president of the Bank of Hawaii in 1989.

"I was named manager of our Waikiki Branch in 1968. At that time I was twenty-seven years old and had been in the bank full time for only five years.

"When I was made manager, Cliff Terry, the president, made it very clear: 'Your big responsibility is to make sure you keep Roy Kelley happy.'

"I asked, 'What do you mean?'

"Cliff said, 'Roy is a big customer, a big depositor. Sometimes he can be a little difficult so I want you to make sure you get off on the right foot.'

"I said I would do that.

"The first week on the job I called Mr. Kelley's office. I expected to have the phone answered by his secretary. Who answers the phone but Mr. Kelley which, at the time, scared me to death. I introduced myself as the new manager of our Waikiki branch and asked if I could come down and spend a few moments with him so I could introduce myself in person.

"He said, 'Sure. Come on down.'

"I asked him, 'Mr. Kelley, where is your office?'

"He said, 'Right here at the Reef Hotel.'

"I asked if there was a room number and he told me just to come to the front desk.

"As I walked down Lewers Road to the Reef Hotel I was nervous as hell. I could still hear the words of Cliff Terry warning me to 'get off on the right foot.' This was a very important meeting for me.

"I walked up to the front desk expecting to be directed to a big office where I would find Roy Kelley sitting behind a big desk in a huge leather chair.

"And, lo and behold, who do I see sitting to the side of the front desk but Mr. Kelley. He is sitting at a little metal desk in a chair with worn-out arms.

"He looks up with a big smile and asked me to sit down. So I walk through a little swinging door which was to the side of the front desk and sit down beside this small metal desk. It is covered with tons of paper strewn all over the place. He had lamp shades and paint cans and fabric samples scattered around the floor.

"We are talking, going through those little things that you go through when you are meeting officially with some-body for the first time.

"But I could tell that his mind was somewhere else. His good eye was on the front desk and he was listening to the conversation that was going on between his front desk manager and a guest, or rather, a prospective guest.

"I wasn't listening to that conversation but I could tell he was, and was preoccupied with what was going on over there.

"Suddenly he says, 'Excuse me, Larry, I need to do something.'

"He jumps up and goes through the swinging door and chases after this young fellow down the lobby who had been at the front desk and he brings him back.

"At that point I turned around to see what was going on.

"What had happened was that this young military fellow on R&R asked for a room and Tony Delpiano had advised this young fellow that he was sorry but the hotel didn't have any rooms left.

"So Roy Kelley brings the fellow back to the front desk and says, 'Tony, we do have a room. Young man, there is a room on the second floor by the pool. The rooms we have there are in the process of being renovated. Now this room doesn't have any rugs on the floor and it doesn't have any drapes but you just want some place to sleep, don't you? You are not after a luxurious room, are you?'

"The young man says, 'No, I just want some place to crash.'

"Roy then says, 'Well, we normally get $24 for this room but we'll give you a rate of $12.50.'

"Well, the young man was delighted and he registered and went off happily to his $12.50 room.

"Roy then turns to Tony and says, 'Now, look, there is $12.50 that we have that we wouldn't have had if you had let that fellow walk out of here. These young fellows just want a place to sleep. They don't care what kind of room they are getting. Sure, we have the rooms under renovation BUT–THE–WORKERS–DON'T–WORK–AT–NIGHT. You have to use your imagination.

"Roy came back to the desk and said, 'Larry, I hope you learned a lesson. If these guys who worked for me owned the hotel, they would think the way I do.'

"That was my introduction to Roy Kelley.

"He was a great negotiator, not only on loans, but on

CDs (Certificates of Deposit). He was also a tough negotiator. I remember one time talking to him on the phone and getting rather philosophical about interest rates: how we structure rates, how we can only pay a certain rate, and why we had to charge him a certain rate.

"In the course of my talk I used the term 'Prime Rate.'

"Roy said, 'Larry, don't talk Prime Rate to me. Prime Rate has no meaning. The only rate I'm interested in is the Roy Kelley Rate.'

"After Cinerama bought the Reef — about a month or so after the takeover of the property — the manager told me an unbelievable story.

"He said that before the end of the first week he was getting calls from guests complaining about smoke in their rooms, rooms that had kitchenettes in them. The guests said that they just couldn't get smoke from the kitchenette out of the rooms.

"Finally, the manager goes up to the rooms to find out what was going on and finds there are hoods and fans in the kitchens. He turns on fans and they work but the smoke doesn't go out.

"The manager calls Roy Kelley and says, 'Mr. Kelley, I have been getting lots of complaints about smoke in the rooms with the kitchenettes. The fan works but the smoke stays in the room.'

"Roy says to him, 'Just tell the guests to open their doors.'

"The manager says he understands that idea but there should be some other way to get the smoke out.

"Roy responds by saying, 'Young man, yes, we have a hood and we have a fan but that doesn't necessarily mean we have pipes from the fan to take the smoke out of the room. When we built those kitchenette rooms, the building inspector said we had to have the hoods and fans, but he didn't say we had to have vents.'

"The manager went back up to one of the rooms and put his hand up behind the vent. It was solid concrete!

"Roy Kelley was a bear on construction costs.

"Once I ran into Roy at Lewers and Kalia Road by the Edgewater.

"At the other corner, a Mainland developer was building a new highrise hotel called The Imperial. It was under construction and Roy grabs me and says, 'Larry, I want to tell you something. See this hotel that is being built? Well, let me tell you the man is crazy. There is no way he can make this hotel pay. Do you know it is costing him $18,000 a room to build this thing? Let me tell you something. If anybody comes to you and wants to borrow money to build a hotel and they say that it is going to cost more than $10,000 a room, you just say, NO!'"

Larry is asked if the story about Mildred Courtney's loan was true.

"Do I remember taking care of Mildred Courtney's loan? Sure. We did that for lots of Roy's employees because he looked after them.

"Lots of people look at Roy Kelley as being an individual who is just out to make money, without much concern for other individuals, but he is not like that at all.

"He and Estelle have literally taken care of hundreds of people in this town.

"Do you remember Dick Edwards, the first manager of the Edgewater Hotel? Well, he went to work for the Breakers Hotel on Beachwalk which was owned by Jimmy Small and Fred Mahoney, but he kept in close touch with the Kelley family after he went to work for the Breakers.

"When he retired, he didn't have much in the way of assets and, when he needed assistance, Roy let him stay in one of the Outrigger hotel penthouses, rent free, until he died several years later.

"I don't believe I have had more respect for any customers than I have had for Roy and Estelle Kelley. They looked after their people."

The Word Gets Out

"I hear you are doing a book on the Kelleys," says Babe Woollett, in the parking lot of the Waialae/Kahala Mall. Babe is a local favorite in the Hawaii travel industry, an English-accented bush pilot, ex-Canadian airline executive, and author of *Have A Banana,* a memory lane book of times that were.

"Let me tell you a Kelley story," he says.

"It must have been in the Sixties and I had arranged a promotion tour on the Mainland for the Royal Fijian Military Band.

"The band was going home via Honolulu and performing on a stop-over in the city and I needed an inexpensive place to bed them down.

"Naturally, I went to see Roy Kelley, who I have known forever, to see if I could get a reduced rate.

"I went to his desk in the lobby of the Reef and explained that I had this low-budget show and needed some help with a favorable hotel rate.

"He just snorted. 'You think I am going to put a bunch of savages in my rooms to poke spears through my hotel walls? Out of the question.'

"I tried one more time, explaining that this was just a two-night stand and they weren't savages and they needed help. Hell, I needed help.

"Roy Kelley's response was that I wasn't right in the mind to get mixed up in such a thing in the first place and even balmier on top of that to try to get a reduced hotel rate.

"'Well, don't get mad about it,' I said, backing off. 'I'll try somewhere else.' And I turned away, discouraged.

"I hadn't gone two steps when this voice roars over my shoulder: 'WOOLLETT, COME BACK HERE. I HAVE KNOWN YOU FOR TEN YEARS, AND YOU ARE JUST AS DUMB NOW AS YOU WERE THEN. *REDUCED RATE!* YOU CAN HAVE THE ROOMS FOR NOTHING, YOU DUMMY.'"

Another. The telephone rings.

It is Andre Tatibouet, chief executive officer of the

locally owned Aston Hotels & Resorts, a company that controls 5,000 hotel rooms in Hawaii, the third largest chain in the Hawaiian hotel industry.

Andre is ten years younger than Richard Kelley but he, too, went to Punahou, made beds, cleaned toilets and carried bags at his mother's first fourteen-room Royal Grove Hotel in Waikiki.

"I hear you are doing a book on the Kelleys," he says. "I want to give you a Kelley vignette.

"I must have been a sophomore in Punahou and wanted to get experience away from my mother's apron strings by working at another hotel. She suggested I talk to Roy Kelley, which I did.

"Mr. Kelley gave me a job on the desk at the original Islander Hotel at a dollar an hour. The hotel was a five-story walk-up. I know because I carried bags up those five flights of stairs. My first tip, I remember, was a dime from a guy who had two heavy bags. My second tip was from a little old lady who gave me a nickel and two pennies.

"Well, I think I went to work on a Wednesday and also worked the weekends. The first Sunday another fellow and I had the duty. I went to work before seven in the morning and the place was dead. There was nothing to do. We poured ourselves some coffee and were standing at the front desk just talking. About ten minutes after seven who walks through the front door but Mr. Kelley himself. He didn't say anything but went straight to a corner where there was a broom and he hauled it out and shoved it towards me, 'Andre,' he said, 'the sidewalk out in front doesn't look like it has been swept in a week. It will give you something to do.'

"He was a very important man by that time in Waikiki and the idea of a man of his position being out and inspecting his hotels at seven on a Sunday morning just floored this teenager.

"I'll never forget it."

A nice twist: The Aston Hotel group has its head office

on the nineteenth floor of the Waikiki Trade Center. The head-quarters building partially occupies the site of the original Islander Hotel where multi-millionaire Andre Tatibouet, former Punahou sophomore, worked carrying bags and sweeping the sidewalk on Sunday mornings.

The phone rings again.

It is Ed Hogan in Newport Beach, California.

Ed Hogan is the head of Pleasant Hawaiian Holidays, the largest tour operator to Hawaii. He also owns several Hawaiian hotels.

"My first real experience with the Kelleys was when I was working with Transocean Airlines, a non-scheduled carrier. I was working in California and succeeded in selling a tour to the Santa Barbara Chamber of Commerce.

"The sales pitch was based on the fact that our DC-4 would leave the Santa Barbara Airport and fly directly to Honolulu. Once there, the tour would stay at the first unit of the new Reef Hotel, just completed right on the beach of Waikiki.

"It was a tremendous sale for me because, if the prestigious Santa Barbara Chamber of Commerce had a successful Hawaiian experience, I could sell similar tours to every Chamber of Commerce in the San Joaquin Valley.

"So I was there to see the plane off and to pray for a great tour.

"Well, I forget if I received a telephone call or a telegram but I remember it was from Howard Steib, the secretary of the Santa Barbara Chamber, who said in effect, 'Delightful here at the Reef Hotel. However, my wife and I have been married many years and are not overly modest people but you have to know we are accustomed to having a door on our bathroom. There is none in the Reef Hotel.'

"Immediately, I got hold of the management at the Reef and asked what the hell was going on.

"The answer was pure Kelley. I was told that there were not only missing bathroom doors but Bill Kline and Jim

Knaefler, part of the management team, were too busy putting down toilet seats on the commodes while the guests were still checking in to get around to such niceties as bathroom doors.

"The hotel wasn't finished yet. They were registering guests at the Edgewater and Roy Kelley had strung an electric line with lightbulbs coming off it across the street so people could find the Reef Hotel.

"I must add that Estelle Kelley was Mrs. Congeniality and when guests saw the owners working sixteen hours a day, they couldn't get too mad.

"It came out all right. The Santa Barbara Chamber made five tours in a row and I sold everybody else in the valley.

"Later, I moved to Honolulu as part of Transocean with my wife and three-month-old child — that was Brian who is now the executive vice president of Pleasant Hawaiian Holidays. We were a young couple, maybe making $1,000 a month, and without a place to live.

"Roy Kelley spat out, 'I have a cottage next to the Edge-water Apartments that you can move into for eight weeks, but then you have to move out because I have four college freshmen coming in.'

"You would have had to hear the rough, commanding tone in his voice to appreciate how tough and intimidating he sounded.

"You see, he was really giving us a free place to live for a couple of months but it was against his nature to sound charitable.

"Later on, Lyle Gusland said that he had a big house out in Kahala and we could move in there for a couple of months while he went to the Mainland and looked for angels to back his new hotels.

"Gus had a free office from Roy Kelley in the basement of the Reef Hotel where Transocean also had an office and I wouldn't be surprised if Roy didn't put a word in his ear.

"Transocean had been started by eleven United Airlines pilots and it did well for a period of time but eventually, it was squeezed out by the big boys.

"I went back to Point Pleasant, New Jersey where my wife and I had met in high school, and started the Pleasant Tour Company. That was thirty-one years ago. On the East Coast there were thousands of travel agencies but they were mostly ethnic oriented, selling trips to people of different nationalities to go back to their home country.

"Nobody knew about Hawaii, so I repeated the Trans-ocean formula, selling Chamber of Commerce tours to the Islands. Eventually, I moved to the West Coast where Fritz Burns, Henry J. Kaiser's partner in housing and shopping centers in California and then the Hawaiian Village Hotel, was my friend and godfather.

"Well, by that time I was Pleasant Hawaiian Holidays and business just grew and grew.

"At one time I had two thousand Hawaiian vacationers in the air every day. One thousand going, one thousand coming.

"The Kelley hotels were my major accommodations source.

"When I got into buying hotels, I always asked Roy Kelley for advice. In 1974, I bought my first hotel, the Kahana Beach between Kaanapali and Napili on Maui. Today, I also own the Kona Hilton on the Big Island, the Sheraton Coconut Beach Hotel on Kauai, the Holiday Isle Hotel in Waikiki — and guess who my landlord is? Right. Roy Kelley.

"Then, in 1982 I bought the Royal Lahaina Hotel for $50 million which gave me nearly six hundred rooms on twenty-seven acres of fee simple property.

"In April, 1990 I signed a management agreement with Dr. Kelley for the Outrigger to take over the Royal Lahaina Hotel. Richard and I have been friends for so many years. He is a wonderful guy with great integrity and a brilliant mind.

"The timing for the Outrigger Royal Lahaina is just perfect."

Dr. Richard Kelley was a frequent visitor to his father's hotel operations while still practicing medicine.

Roy Kelley shares the building details with Dr. Richard Kelley on completing the Reef Towers in the background.

Roy and Estelle share a kiss and a glass of
champagne over a "Kelleyland" cake at Roy
Kelley's sixtieth birthday party.

Headlines forecast the sale of three Kelley hotels to Cinerama.

Roy Kelley takes the front seat in the St. Patrick's Day Parade.
Passengers sitting behind him are Ernie Albrecht, George Murphy, and Jack Riley.

Dick Edwards, the first manager of the Edgewater Hotel,
receives a book from Roy Kelley.

The veterans of the trenches.
Left to right, Tom Burke, Tony Delpiano,
Chuck Comeau, Mildred Courtney.

Dick Norstrom in front of the first
of many Outrigger Shops.

Genial Al Batz of the Brass Rail poses with
Estelle and Roy under the screaming eagle
insignia of his 101st Airborne Division.

Relaxing on Diamond
Head, Richard Kelley,
Outrigger's CEO and
David Carey, president,
stand behind their
respective wives,
Linda V.G. Kelley and
Kathryn Kelley Carey.

In 1989, the Outrigger Hotels Hawaii established a $10,000 annual scholarship in honor of Estelle Louise Kelley for students in Kapiolani Community College. Here, Estelle Kelley is surrounded by family and friends at the announcement party.

Front row (L to R): Chuck Kelley, Susan Rolles, Richard Kelley, Linda V.G. Kelley, Roy C. Kelley, Estelle L. Kelley, Jean Rolles, Estelle M. Kelley, Michelle Norstrom, Provost Morgan (KCC). Back row: Bitsy Kelley Black, Jenny Kelley, Pat Kelley, Kiki Tidwell, Colleen Kelley, Scott Rolles, Pete Petrequin, David Carey.

Sunday morning in the Kelley
penthouse. Estelle Kelley
prepares her famous Sunday
morning waffles.

Some things never change.
Roy Kelley still takes care of
his pigeons after his daily
morning swim in the Pacific
Ocean off Waikiki Beach.

CHAPTER TEN

Maintaining Traditions ...
The New Management ...
The Future

The 1980s marked the retirement of Roy and Estelle Kelley from active management in the Outrigger Hotels in Hawaii.

Their involvement became confined to daily luncheons with family, friends, and advisers where current projects, the state of business and, occasionally, a choice rumor are discussed.

The second generation of the Kelleys had also changed.

Pat Kelley sold her travel business to the parent company and started a new company called "Mother of the Bride" which advises and assists people who want to be married in Hawaii. Confined to bed by a serious illness, Pat continued her nonprofit marriage bureau in her usual high spirits while flat on her back.

Pat's husband, Jerry Petrequin, has become coordinator of corporate contributions for Outrigger Hotels Hawaii.

Jeannie Rolles, who won her hotel degree in 1975 from Cornell, returned to the family corporation. Today, she is vice president, Property Management, supervising over three hundred leases on shops, restaurants, and bars within the hotels and controlling the rental of approximately a hundred and fifty apartment units.

In the best Kelley tradition, she works a seven-day week but, also in the Kelley tradition, she takes vacations away from the telephone. She goes hiking in jungles, canoeing down rivers, backpacking and horsepacking in mountains, and skiing in exotic places.

Dr. Richard Kelley has become the chairman and chief executive officer.

It has been an arduous, demanding twenty years for Richard. Assuming control of the Kelley empire has required new skills. His learning curve looks like a ski jump in reverse.

But, if Roy Kelley was the successful, explosive wildcatter with the right instincts for sniffing out potentially profitable hotel sites, Richard Kelley is the cool, intellectual surgeon capable of advancing the Outrigger fortunes with calculated financial moves across a breakfront of hotels, real estate, investments, and services.

Hawaii has boomed in those twenty years and the Outrigger Hotels have kept ahead of the marketplace, thanks to Richard's newly honed abilities as a hotelier/financier.

The turning point could well have been the Prince Kuhio Hotel in 1982.

A major change in the traditional Kelley hotel profile came when Richard Kelley bought the Prince Kuhio Hotel, a 626-room hotel on Kuhio Avenue.

The Prince Kuhio was built as a luxury hotel, but, being off the beach, had never attained the level of occupancy to make it sufficiently profitable.

"It was all Richard's show," Roy Kelley said.

The cigar box was no longer big enough to handle such transactions.

Richard remembers: "We financed about two-fifths of the Prince Kuhio acquisition.

"We bought the Prince Kuhio for $40 million which

comes out to about $63,000 a room. The rule of thumb is that we would have to price those rooms at $63 per night, on average, to make a profit.

"When we took it over, we charged $27 and $30 a night just to get bodies in there and help establish the name. We did take some losses but we also gradually increased the rates. We passed the $63-a-night average a couple of years ago.

"Also, the Prince Kuhio had extensive food and beverage facilities. We accepted that challenge and probably rate ourselves a B-plus on how we handled it.

"We have an excellent Trellises Restaurant there which we are quite proud of. It's making a profit. The banquet department also gets high marks.

"Originally, there was a fine dining room in the basement called The Protea. We couldn't make it go. The food and service were absolutely elegant but there was a limited market and, being in a basement, it had tough competition against restaurants with great views like Michel's and John Dominis. We closed it.

"Compadres took it as a concession but they had a tough time and finally decided they couldn't make a go of it either.

"We may take a run at it again.

"Trellises is the only restaurant we totally operate by ourselves. The other restaurants are run by a manager who is on an incentive arrangement. The employees are ours. The liquor license is ours. If the manager makes a profit, he shares in the profit. If he has a loss, that loss is carried forward until he makes a profit. This is definitely a product of my father's thinking and it is highly motivating."

The question arises that, since the Kelley hotels were built on a traditional formula of MWA (Management by Walking Around) and (MSFD) Management by Standing by the Front Desk, how is it possible to maintain this successful format with so many hotels?

"We're trying to do a blend there," replies Richard.

"Although I don't do it anymore on a daily basis, I don't think there is a week that goes by that I am not behind some front desk talking to a customer. And I'm always talking to employees.

"Yesterday I spent two hours down in the bowels of the laundry room talking to the laundry workers, to the supervisors, and to the manager ... just getting a feel for what was going on.

"I found out that the laundry was producing gray linen. The problem was that the personnel department was not putting enough people in the laundry room. The people had to do more work than they could handle and were loading a hundred and fifty pounds of laundry in a machine designed to take a hundred and twenty-five pounds. You only know this by talking to the guy loading the machine.

"We changed that the same morning.

"I went into a reservation office of one of our hotels where the manager was off at a meeting in Toronto. I walked in on the girl who was doing rooms control and it was obvious that vital changes needed to be made in the system she was using, so we made the changes right there.

"It's very important to manage that way. Look at Crandall of American Airlines. He does it. He goes out on the ramp. Out on the flight lines. Talks to the mechanics, to the baggage loaders. Finds out what is actually going on in the company.

"This was 'Housekeepers' Week' in our hotels so I made three separate morning trips to Leonard's Bakery and bought fresh malasadas and took them down to various housekeeping groups, just to chat with them.

"You've got to be able to get with the men and women running the operation.

"One reason we have been so successful is because we stay so close to our operations.

"In today's market I see a lot of hotel owners doing very badly because they are not also the managers. As an owner/ manager, we can make decisions quickly. We can take a loss tomorrow morning when we have to take a loss in order to make money next week.

"We need to extend our executive talent so the operation is really not so dependent on David Carey, who is now the president, and me. We need to spend time concentrating on taking the company to the next step."

What is the next step?

"We are continuing to look at expansion to the neighbor islands and on the Mainland.

"On the Mainland we have established Outrigger Lodging Services which presently manages five hotels, one of which we own, in Fort Worth. The Fort Worth property was in foreclosure to an insurance company so we were able to get an attractive purchase arrangement.

"John Fitts, formerly the president of Colony Hotels, is the manager of Outrigger Lodgings. He's a fifty-fifty partner, continuing on another tradition my father started, that of partnerships.

"We will continue to be investors in real estate. We seem to know the hotel business so I think we will continue to invest in hotels and use our expertise to get value out of the hotels.

"For example, in the last five years we bought the Hobron and the Malia with a hundred percent financing and turned around this last year and sold them for a substantial profit."

In 1989, the Outrigger Hotels sold six out of seven properties we had put on the market earlier, but the Outrigger condition of sale was a ten-year management contract on each property.

All the properties were sold to Japanese investors.

It appeared to observers that the sales accomplished several purposes.

In 1989, the Hawaii leisure market was at a peak. If, as in the past, the tourist business were cyclical, it would be the most opportune time to sell, repeating the timing of the Cinerama sale.

By selling to Japanese owners, Outrigger strengthened its marketing ties to the Japanese segment of the Hawaii tourist market which accounts for almost twenty percent of the annual visitor count.

An important third fact was the major cash asset engendered by the sales. The cash allowed the Outrigger Hotels to finance a $100 million refurbishing program without going to the banks. In a real sense, it was the proverbial Kelley cigar box financing.

Traditionally, the Kelley hotels were famous for "a clean room and a good bed," but not necessarily their maintenance. One story told within the family is of a couple who returned to the same room in the Reef for seven years. Always requested the same room. On their first visit, they noted a lamp shade in their room had a burn on one side. The second year, the burned shade was still there. On every subsequent return, the first thing they did when they checked into the room was to check the lamp shade to see if the burn was still there. It always was.

Another in-house maintenance story has it that when the Reef Hotel got new carpeting, their old rugs went to the Islander, whose old rugs went to the Ala Wai Terrace.

Everybody was happy because everybody got better rugs.

The Coming Generations

What is the policy of a closely held family-owned corporation about hiring siblings?

"We are in the point of transition, working out a policy," answers Richard.

"Jeannie and Pat and I were all expected to work in the business. Without any particular plan, Pat started a tour desk, Jeannie really got involved with her husband in restaurants, and I fell into the hotel management end of it.

"Now there are eleven grandchildren and probably an equal number of great grandchildren.

"Jeannie had a son, Scott, who is a successful restaurateur, and a daughter, Kiki. Pat had two daughters, Estelle, who is an attorney, and Michelle.

"I had five children with Jane, my first wife. Kathryn, the

eldest, is married to David Carey. My son, Charles — or Chuck — is a board certified physician. Linda Jane is now Linda Jane Springmeier, and Elizabeth, is Bitsy Kelley Black. My last child by my first marriage is Mary Colleen.

"After Jane's death in Arizona, I remarried in 1979 to Linda Van Gilder. She and I have had two children: Christopher who is seven and Anne Marie who is four.

"The Kelley tradition extended to Linda. Shortly after we were married, she left her teaching position at Punahou to learn the hotel business. And, in typical family fashion, she rotated through various departments until she founded a much-needed Risk Management Department for the growing Outrigger chain. She ran the department until the birth of Anne Marie, when she retired to take care of the children.

"We hired an outside consultant who specializes in developing programs for family-held corporations to help us work toward the best solutions.

"The consultant identifies mother and father as G-Ones, or the first generation. Jeannie, Pat and I are G-Twos. Our children are G-Threes and the great-grandchildren are G-Fours.

"Families who are in business together have a lot of problems, opportunities, and challenges. One of the natural problems is the employment of family members.

"Too often, you get an incompetent relative pushed into a job.

"To avoid that, we have adopted the policy that if a family member wants to work in the Outrigger Hotels he has to have had a minimum college level education and outside experience in the industry before he can enter the company.

"He would have to have had a minimum of two years outside experience and at least one advancement on that job.

"Only then can he apply for a job with the Outrigger Hotels, and then there has to be a job opening. We will not create a job. He will get paid and treated like everybody else.

"The only exceptions are the Summer Fun jobs.

"The Summer Fun program has turned out to be quite large. We actually take on about seventy-five students every summer.

"We try to give preference to local kids interested in a hotel career. We probably have more people from Pearl City High and Kamehameha Schools than we do from Punahou.

"Then, we also have a smattering of students from Mainland colleges because we feel they bring something extra into the mix."

"Various G-Threes have worked in the hotels over the years. Today my daughter, Bitsy, is the only one employed. She is in a management training program.

"Also, my oldest daughter's husband, David Carey, is my right-hand man. We are lucky to have him."

In October, 1988, David Carey was named president of Outrigger Hotels Hawaii.

David became the first G-Three in a command post.

Any thought of family nepotism is quickly dispelled after but a short conversation with William David Puterbaugh Carey III.

He is a law-sharp, hotel-oriented young man who gives the instant impression of being able — confidently able — to isolate and analyze any problem and move swiftly toward a solution.

David Carey was born in Denver, Colorado, in 1955. He is a tall (six-one) lean athlete who plays soccer three times a week. His moustached face is usually somber and intense, except when it breaks out into a 300-watt smile.

After graduating from Stanford where he met Kathy and, after working for a year in every department of the Outrigger Hotels, he returned to the University of Santa Clara to earn his law degree and then his master's degree in business.

"My great grandfather, Emerson Carey, lived in Hutchinson, Kansas, where he started the Carey Salt Company from the big vein of salt that runs through the middle of Kansas. He chose to name his oldest son William David Puterbaugh Carey.

"I went to South Denver High where I had straight A's during my four years and made the All City Golf Team.

"I wanted to continue to play golf and decided to pick a college in the sunbelt so I could play all year long. I only applied to one school, Stanford, and with my grades, outside activities," David stops and adds with a smile, "plus the fact that my neighbor's bridge partner was Denver's Stanford rep, I was in.

"At Stanford, I liked math and science and was inclined toward engineering, but I learned that if you wanted to play on the golf team, it meant a lot of traveling. That meant you needed to take courses where all you had to do was read the assigned books, do the papers, and show up for the exam.

"But math and science and engineering courses meant attending classes three times a week, classes you couldn't afford to miss.

"It was then that I made my first destiny decision, deciding, maybe, I wasn't a Nicklaus or a Watson and that I was paying a lot of money for an education at Stanford. I stopped playing competitive golf and started taking school seriously.

"By my junior year, I pretty much knew that I was going to be an electrical engineer because I was interested in stereos and electronics and it was my opinion that we were coming into the semiconductor age. And there were a lot of great things going on at Stanford at that time in terms of electronics.

"That same year I went home with a fellow classmate. His father was an engineer with Aerojet, a major defense contractor, and there was a huge cut in defense contracts that resulted in a layoff of almost the entire division where my friend's father worked.

"So, here you have a suburb of Sacramento where there are lots of engineers with two kids in college, nice houses with mortgages and two cars ... and half of them are out of jobs. Who's going to hire a forty-five-year-old engineer at a top salary when you could hire a guy fresh out of school for half the money?

"That had a real impact on me."

David puts his hands behind his head and stares at the ceiling, reliving that moment in time.

"Then I worked in an electronic shop over the summer with a guy in his forties who said that the engineering he learned in college was completely obsolete and, as a matter of fact, the engineering he learned five years ago was completely obsolete. He said to stay abreast of the field you had to spend an enormous amount of time studying. Just to stay even.

"I was too far into the program to change so I kept with it, although I always wanted to become involved with management.

"Then, in my junior year, I was playing soccer and, I remember, one day on the soccer field seeing two girls on the sidelines who had made the freshmen men's team because there was no women's soccer program at Stanford at that time. Naturally, everybody knew who they were but I had not met either one of them.

"Well, one of them was Kathy, who I met later on at a frat party.

"We hit it off fairly well and went out together for about a year.

"Toward the end of the semester, she said one day, 'Why don't you come out and visit me sometime this summer in Hawaii.'

"And I said, 'Sure, that sounds great. I've never been to Hawaii.'

"So near the end of summer I came out to Hawaii for a little over a week. I thought it was terrific. I just loved the climate. I remember sitting on the seawall in front of Kelley's house on Diamond Head about ten o'clock one night when the moon was about thirty-five degrees above the water. There were these little waves coming into the shore and with just enough wind so you could still see the reflection of the moon across the water and I remember asking Kathy, 'Is this what it's like all year round?'

"The answer was, 'Oh, yes.'

"I said, 'This is for me.'

"Before the week was out I had asked Richard for a job. I said that I was graduating from Stanford the coming year and

I would like to come out to Hawaii and work in one of his hotels.

"I had no idea of the scope of the Kelley operations at that time. I just knew they had a couple of hotels and it sounded like a fun job. You know, an eight-hour shift where you didn't have to work too hard and you could go surfing and play golf and all that good stuff."

David snorts at his own naivete.

"I obviously wasn't aware of the Kelley work ethic. But I was to learn.

"After graduation I came over and started to work. Kathy still had two years of university left and, while we were close, we weren't super close. Neither one of us had it in mind that our relationship was a long-term thing.

"Well, I started working at the front desk at the Outrigger West, then Outrigger East. I did the cashiering at the Waikiki Village, then I did a stint as the assistant manager.

"I did some relief managing for people and did the night audit for a while and then went over and worked in reservations and then did rooms control for a bit.

"I worked with Richard on all of our wholesale contracts, blocking out rooms for the coming year, which is a major portion of our business. I got involved with the computers and would go over to Richard's office and read through the computer manuals and try out the different programs.

"I did this on my own because it interested me. I was only getting enough money to pay the rent, buy the groceries and the other small expenses.

"Then I got involved in group tour contracts while also doing support work for Richard on a couple of company tax cases.

"In each instance we were always having to go down to the lawyer's office. We had to go see the lawyer about everything and I started thinking that maybe that was the way society was going. The only guys who ever won were the lawyers. It was true then and it is true today.

"Richard was a big believer in education. When I started talking about going to law school, he pushed me on. So I applied to several law schools, took the exams and finally chose the University of Santa Clara which was just down the highway from Stanford.

"I was about halfway through the law program when I decided to add on the MBA program, a master's degree in business administration. It meant doubling up courses for a while but I took the full law program. I'm happy I did.

"Law school was the biggest eye opener for me.

"First of all, as an engineering and math major, I had avoided writing as if it were the plague.

"But law school forced me to write in order to survive. Every day I had to turn in a full page brief on every case we studied. That first semester was tremendously painful because I had no practice or skill in written communications. In the end, it was the best thing in the world for me.

"The other thing about law school was that we were reading three to five case histories per class. With five classes, five times a week, that meant between a hundred to a hundred, twenty-five case histories a week.

"Each case involved a ton of different things, the size of the business involved, the problem, the issue, the arguments for and against. It's amazing how much you learn about society and life and business in general just by reading legal case histories.

"Kathy, in the meantime, had graduated from Stanford and had come down to get an MBA at Santa Clara. She got her undergraduate degree at the same time I finished my first year of law school and we came back to Hawaii and got married. That was 1979.

"The first summer in law school I came back and worked in the hotels. My job that summer was to produce the first guest services directory that the hotels had ever commissioned. They had never had a service directory before. They just didn't believe in spending money on things like that.

"It provided me with a fundamental hotel education because I had to go around to every shop and service and figure out what they were doing. I talked to bellmen and housekeepers and the front desk personnel. I had them write down the ten to fourteen most common guest questions. Before I was through, I knew more about the Kelley hotels than anyone, except Richard.

"I graduated from the law program that year and the business program the next year and then went to work for the Carlsmith law firm in downtown Honolulu where I did a lot of corporate work, including work on the takeover of the Crown Corporation by the Watkins Pacific group.

"One of my most fascinating assignments was working with the members of the Dillingham family when the Dillingham Corporation was being bought out. It gave me a tremendous overview of inter-family issues and the impact of estate planning for different branches of the family. Illuminating. At the end, I had to get sixty-five different people to sign off on the structure of the deal.

"I worked on the private placement of macadamia nut farms on the Big Island for C. Brewer and then Richard called me one day and says, 'We're thinking of buying this hotel in Waikiki and I wonder if you could come down for a meeting in Roy's office.'

"Well, I went down there and they were all set to sign up a deal to buy the Prince Kuhio, the first time the Kelley's had bought such a major facility.

"It was very clear to me that Roy was fixed on buying the property. His basic theory was that it was not feasible to build anymore in Waikiki, but here was an asset where the guy running the hotel was almost bankrupt and the deal was on the table and it was going to be a good one in the long run. According to Roy Kelley, the price was $40-million and 'piss on the details.'

"I remember it was a difficult situation for me to get Richard, but especially Roy, comfortable with the idea that, hey, this deal is different and you don't sign a $40 million deal on a paper napkin. You really need to do some serious legal work to make a deal of such magnitude work correctly.

"Well, they wanted to close in two weeks which was

really unusual for a transaction of that size. I succeeded in getting the deadline extended.

"So I basically knocked myself out for about six weeks working until eight, nine, ten o'clock every night. There were unbelievable complex problems including the union problem — because the Prince Kuhio was a union hotel — so we had to go through some very eye-opening stuff.

"The labor strategy worked and, although it was a little bumpy, we got the result we wanted.

"Since I have been around, the purchase of the Prince Kuhio was the most significant because it was a luxury hotel.

"There were lots of questions asked around the community about what was going to happen when the Kelleys took over the Prince Kuhio."

David ticks off the problems on his extended fingers, one at a time.

"Were they going to make it another low ball hotel? Were they going to contract out the food and beverage? Were they going to let the place run down? Were they going to fill the lobby with shops? The property was already losing money, what was going to happen?

"I remember, distinctly, Richard Kelley standing up at a press conference — the first time he had faced a heated press situation. He did okay, but to listen to him speaking today is to hear an amazing transition.

"From that time forward Richard became the public leader and the family spokesman on everyday decisions.

"Up to that time it was Roy's pressure or influence that said let's buy this building and let's buy it at this price.

"Even in the case of the Prince Kuhio, I tried to get Roy to let me negotiate the price down a little bit. You know, $40 million should have a little fat in it. But he said, 'No, I set the price and that's the way I want to do it.'

"I got a call the day we closed the deal from two people saying, 'Gee, we thought we had that deal. Would you consider a million dollars for flipping it?'

"So you never know. Roy was probably right.

"In order to buy the hotel, the Kelleys had to take out their first major real estate mortgage. It was about $26 million.

"Then the next deal that came up was taking the Formans and Cinerama out of the hotel business which, as it stood, wasn't a good deal.

"We had to restructure, renegotiate, and buy back the properties to make economic sense for the Kelleys.

"Another major issue was that Cinerama had all union employees and we had to integrate them into the nonunion Outrigger system.

"So this was another major financial commitment at the same time as the Prince Kuhio transaction.

"We had to suck every resource from every corner of the Kelley empire to make it all happen, which we did.

"That's when I discovered that the Kelleys had entities all over the place. Corporations, partnerships, loans, advances.

"Well, Roy was not into any financial organization at all. Roy said if the money is in the cash register — the cigar box theory in capsule — then everything was okay.

"He knew, absolutely, from day to day where the money was. He knew when things were going well, or not so well. Accounting systems and financial statements were not really meaningful to him.

"Richard, on the other hand, brought in computers, introduced financial statements.

"About then, with my lawyer's hat on, I told Richard that I thought we really needed to take an overall look at the Kelley family economic environment.

"Richard let me have six weeks when I went through every file in their filing system, every trust, every will, every deed, every lease, all the corporate and partnership files until I pretty well knew where all the pieces in the Kelley pie were.

"At that time, the government was about to pass a law that prevented interest-free loans between related parties. That would have caused a major problem for the Kelley system because, until that time, it was just a matter of taking it out of one pocket and putting it in another pocket.

"The Reef Hotel was in need of major renovations but where was the money going to come from? The entity that owned it didn't have the resources. But the resources were available over here in another entity.

"The ownership of the Kelley Hotels involved a bunch of outside partners.

"So, with a tax attorney, we were able to develop a plan for reorganization, putting all the Kelley entities into a single pot so that the company could utilize its financial strength.

"Systematically, we set out on a program of buying out all of the non-Kelley-family ownerships and consolidating them into a single organization. We finished in 1985 with one big pile under the name of Outrigger Hotels Hawaii.

"By then, we had a reorganized entity with a single balance sheet and tremendous financial power.

"However, in my view, the administrative structure behind the new organization was just not there. The finance and accounting departments were not strong enough. The business was getting bigger and more complex and Richard was working unbelievable hours.

"That's when he made me an offer I couldn't refuse. I went to work directly for the company.

"My title was executive vice president and general counsel. Besides being in charge of legal work, I also had a major hand in all of the business and finance transactions, risk management and insurance, human resources and computers, and back-of-the-house stuff.

"My goal was to rebuild the back of the house. We redid the financial systems. We had never audited financial statements because we were so fragmented. We do now.

"We redid the computer systems and the reservations system.

"Then I began to experience frustration. We had all of these administrative departments organized and were going forward but our marketing and operations were not on the same wave length. They were not moving forward at the same pace as the rest of the departments.

"But, fortunately for me, that's when — last year — Richard made me president. My new responsibilities included marketing and operations.

"Last year we broke every record there was. We had record sales and record occupancies.

"Our sales this year will top $160 million, maybe $165."

An observer, familiar with the successful Kelley tradition of standing by the front desk, is curious how a new, dynamic management is going to maintain the format.

David heaves a sigh, "Well, you are forced to change the format. The sheer size of the organization, the numbers, won't allow it.

"My long-term theory is to develop a team of what I call warm and fuzzy managers, capable of maintaining what we call the *ohana* ("family") feeling, and the *aloha* spirit.

"We have set it right out as one of our corporate objectives. If your hard ass doesn't fit into that warm and fuzzy mold, your hard ass is not going to fit into our organization. Managers will also have to be diligent, hands-on managers.

"To a certain extent we have to experience a transition. Where Roy knew every single employee, to Richard knowing most of the employees, to me knowing most of the managers, has to be a fact of life with a company owning so many hotels.

"I make a point of seeing every property at least once a month and we hold a series of round table discussions where we invite different employees to come in to talk with us, ask questions, volunteer ideas. There are no supervisors or managers around.

"It's amazing what they tell you is going on, and, if they don't, you can read in-between the lines.

"We now can have 15,000 visitors in our hotels on any night so guest contact by the Kelleys is really impossible.

"We believe in putting a smart person on the front desk to make sure the guest is taken care of. We believe that still distinguishes us from the competition.

"We make a real effort to keep the family feeling, the ohana feeling. We are reminded of it every time a guest comes in and says, 'One thing about your hotel is that people are so nice."

How does W. David P. Carey III, president of Outrigger Hotels Hawaii, view the future?

"I think we either grow or die and it is hard to grow anymore in Waikiki. So we look to the neighbor islands. We are going to continue to grow on the Mainland where we find the right opportunities.

"We feel, in Hawaii, we understand the Asian and Down Under markets and will probably be looking in those directions.

"I view the hotel industry like the airline industry a few years ago when there were lots of small airlines around. Then there was this tremendous focus toward consolidation and there are only so many major airlines around today.

"I see this happening in the hotel industry. The major chains will become even larger because it takes that kind of marketing clout to break through the haze of marketing messages to reach the potential customers.

"We need to acquire marketing or management control over properties *now*. The opportunities are *now*.

"Our company has, historically, been opportunistic. Buying the Prince Kuhio was an example. Buying and selling the Outrigger Malia, the Outrigger Maile Court, and the Outrigger Hobron while maintaining the management control were other examples.

"We have tremendous financial strength now which allows us to capitalize on opportunities.

"That gives us the extended opportunity to diversify economically. After all, the Kelley eggs are entirely in one Waikiki basket and, while that is a wonderful investment, one Hurricane Hugo or one major tidal wave could put the entire investment at a major economic risk. So it makes economic sense to diversify that investment geographically.

"Look for diversification as a future activity.

"And look for us to grow. We aren't going to die."

Outrigger Hotels Hawaii is poised to move aggressively into the Mainland market with its corporate treasury where Mainland hotels can be bought at the rate of $40,000 a room as opposed to $90,000 a room in Hawaii.

"The last decade of the Twentieth Century is going to be the beginning of a new era for The Outrigger," says Richard Kelley.

"We have new Japanese owners to report to as a management company and they constitute new clients to satisfy.

"We are going to have to develop new markets and consider how we are going to position ourselves before the potentially new guests in these markets.

"We have new properties to appraise, obtain and develop.

"It is going to be an exciting decade."

EPILOGUE

The final page of the story comes with the latest photo entered into the family album.

The photo shows Estelle and Roy Kelley standing under the Chinese Moon Gate on the terrace of their penthouse apartment in the Outrigger Waikiki Tower.

They are holding a plaque.

On October 27, 1989 in Miami, Florida, Roy and Estelle Kelley, founders of Outrigger Hotels Hawaii, were awarded the American Society of Travel Agents' highest honor — induction into the ASTA Hall of Fame.

The award, one of the most prestigious in the travel industry, was accepted by Dr. Richard Kelley, chairman and CEO of Outrigger Hotels Hawaii, on behalf of his parents.

"My parents," Richard told his audience, "are in their eighties. They had to choose between an eleven-hour flight to Miami or their daily swim in the Pacific Ocean off Waikiki Beach. So they have sent me to accept this honor and to express to you their deepest gratitude."

Over 6,000 travel agents and travel industry officials attended the ASTA World Travel Congress in Miami, Florida, where the Kelleys were honored for their role in making Hawaii available to middle-income travelers and for their work with travel agents.

"For over thirty years my parents were active in ASTA and during that time enjoyed many special friendships and benefits from fellow members," Richard noted.

"Roy and Estelle Kelley nurtured relationships with our travel agents friends very carefully. They placed heavy emphasis on integrity, consistency, and efficiency in honoring these relationships, an emphasis which we in the family will continue to honor."

While the plaque Roy and Estelle are holding acknowledges their entry into the ASTA Hall of Fame, it takes just a small flight of fantasy to convert it into an "Horatio Alger Award," whose inscription summarizing their attainment of the American Dream, might logically be taken directly from one of Horatio Alger's most popular book titles: **"Pluck and Luck."**

CHRONOLOGY
OF EXISTING OUTRIGGER HOTELS

HOTEL NAME	COMPLETION DATE	PURCHASE DATE	SOLD DATE	REPURCHASED DATE
Outrigger Ala Wai Terrace	1947			
Outrigger Edgewater	1951		1969	1978
Outrigger Edgewater Lanais	1955			
Outrigger Reef (Ocean and Diamond Head Towers)	1955		1969	1984
Outrigger Reef Pacific Tower	1958			
Outrigger Reef Towers	1959		1969	1984
Outrigger Coral Seas	1960			
Outrigger Reef Lanais	1962			
Outrigger Waikiki Surf West	1962		1989	
Outrigger Reef *Pacific Tower*	1965		1969	1984
Outrigger Waikiki	1967			

HOTEL NAME	COMPLETION DATE	PURCHASE DATE	SOLD DATE	REPURCHASED DATE
Outrigger Surf East	1969		1989	
Outrigger Waikiki Surf	1970		1989	
Outrigger Surf	1972			
Outrigger East	1972			
Outrigger West	1973			
Outrigger Village	1974			
Outrigger Waikiki Tower	1978			
Outrigger Prince Kuhio		1982		
Outrigger Malia		1984	1989	
Outrigger Seaside Suites	1985			
Outrigger Hobron		1986	1989	
Outrigger Maile Court		1986	1989	

VISITOR COUNT
TO HAWAII BY YEAR

1929   22,000

Roy & Estelle Kelley arrive in Hawaii aboard the
City of Los Angeles. Travel time: 7 days.

1938   23,000

Pan American Airlines link Hawaii to North America
Travel time: 18 hours.

1947   25,000

The Kelleys open their first hotel: The Islander Hotel.

1951   50,000

United Airlines introduce 4-engine aircraft on
California/Hawaii route. Travel time: 8 hours.

1955   108,000

Henry J. Kaiser opens the Hawaiian Village Hotel.

1959   300,000

Hawaii granted statehood in March.
First jets fly to Hawaii. Travel time: 5 hours.

1967   1,000,000

Outrigger Waikiki opens.

1970   2,000,000

First jumbo jets arrive with capacity of over
400 passengers each.

1976   3,000,000

Visitor count continues to increase dramatically,
thanks to expanded airline routes and new hotels.

1982   4,000,000

Visitor spending creates $448,000 in tax
revenues and supports over 160,000 jobs.

1986   5,000,000

Hawaii's image is sold in every corner of
the world, thanks to the marketing efforts of
airlines, hotels, and the Hawaii Visitors Bureau.

1989   6,500,000

Japan is Hawaii's number two market,
accounting for about 20% of all visitors.

I N D E X

J ohn W. McDermott is in a second career as a travel book author. A resident of Hawaii since 1951, he worked, managed, and eventually owned a major Honolulu advertising agency with many clients in the travel business.

He sold the agency in 1975 to turn to travel writing and has since written ten travel experience books in a series titled *"How to get Lost and Found in ---"*. Destinations have included Fiji, Tahiti, the Cook Islands, Australia, Japan, California, Hawaii, London and two books on New Zealand.

As a direct participant in the Hawaii travel market and, later, as a professional travel writer, he has been a close observer of the mushrooming Kelley success.

"One of the great parts of the story is the sweet, complete, untouched attitude of the Kelleys about their multi-million dollar status. I think that their only regret is that life isn't longer so they could do it all again," McDermott writes.